ADVANCED ENGLISH

Course Book

Level 6

SCHOLASTIC
New York Toronto London Auckland
Sydney New Delhi Hong Kong

Page 147 constitutes an extension of the copyright page.

Published by Scholastic India Pvt. Ltd.
A subsidiary of Scholastic Inc. New York, 10012 (USA).
Publishers since 1920, with international operations in Canada, Australia, New Zealand, the United Kingdom, India, and Hong Kong.

For information regarding permission, write to:
Scholastic India Pvt. Ltd.
A-27, Ground Floor, Bharti Sigma Centre,
Infocity-I, Sector-34, Gurgaon 122001 (India)

Series editor: Aishwarya Subramanian
Layout, design and typesetting by Ram Das Lal

First edition: September 2010
Reprint: December 2010; September 2011; March 2012; March; November 2013; January ; November 2015 ; November 2017

ISBN-13: 978-81-8477-497-9

Printed at Shivam Offset Press, New Delhi

The Lexile measure represents the complexity of the text. This Lexile measure—along with other characteristics of the text, such as developmental level and subject matter—helps in selecting books that best match a reader's level and goals. For more information on using lexile measure to connect readers with test, visit www.Lexile.com

Contents

A Child's Right to Read 5

Detailed Table of Contents 6

Introduction 8

Growing Up

In the Playground 13

The Schoolboy 20

Dear Dad 23

Family

Brother and Sister 33

A Martian Homecoming 36

History

The Date for Reform 47

Rajyasri and Her Brothers 53

Ozymandias 59

The Sea 62

Words

Why Books are Dangerous 69

Horsemail 74

Pretty Words 79

Science

When the Martians Landed 85

Elevators and Escalators 92

Science Star Omar 96

Nature

The Caged Thrush Freed and Home Again 107

The Man Who Wanted to Fly 110

Life Before the Dinosaurs 124

Sports

The Trial 133

The Spirit of Cricket 141

Acknowledgements 147

Evaluation Table 148

We believe that LITERACY – the ability to READ, WRITE and UNDERSTAND – is the BIRTHRIGHT of every child in the world as well as the pathway to SUCCEED in school and to realize a complete life. Young people need to read NONFICTION for INFORMATION to understand their world, and LITERATURE for IMAGINATION to understand themselves. • We believe that the massive amounts of DIGITAL information and IMAGES now transmitted daily make it even more important for a young person to know how to ANALYZE, INTERPRET and understand information, to separate FACT from OPINION, and to have deep RESPECT for LOGICAL THINKING. • We believe that literature and DRAMA, whether on printed pages, screens, on stage or film, help young people EXPERIENCE the GREAT STORIES of EMOTION and ACTION, leading to a deeper UNDERSTANDING of what it means to be TRULY HUMAN. Without this literacy heritage, life lacks MEANING, COHERENCE and SOUL. • We believe every child has a right to a "textual lineage" – a reading and writing autobiography which shows that WHO YOU ARE is in part developed through the STORIES and INFORMATION you've experienced. This textual lineage will enable all young people to have a READING AND WRITING IDENTITY which helps them understand who they are and how they can MAKE THEIR LIVES BETTER. In short, "YOU ARE WHAT YOU READ." • We believe every child should have ACCESS to books, magazines, newspapers, computers,

A Child's Right to Read

e-readers, and text on phones. Whatever way you read, you will need to figure out what the FACTS are or what the STORY tells you. No matter how and where you get access to IDEAS, you will need the SKILLS of READING to UNDERSTAND yourself and YOUR WORLD. • We believe that reading WIDELY and reading FLUENTLY will give children the reading STAMINA to deal with more CHALLENGING texts they will meet in college, at work and in everyday LIFE. And every child should be able to CHOOSE and own the books they want to read, for that choice builds LITERACY CONFIDENCE – the ability to read, WRITE and SPEAK about what they know, what they feel, and who they are. • We believe that every child has the right to a great teacher who will help them LEARN to read and LOVE TO READ. Children need teachers who provide INTENTIONAL, focused INSTRUCTION to give young people the skills to read and INTERPRET INFORMATION or UNDERSTAND GREAT STORIES they will encounter throughout life. • We believe that in the 21st century, the ability to read is NECESSARY not only to SUCCEED but to SURVIVE—for the ability to UNDERSTAND information and the POWER of stories is the key to a life of PURPOSE and MEANING.

Growing Up	Lesson	Reading Comprehension	Vocabulary
	In the Playground (610L)	Questions and answers	Reporting words
	The Schoolboy	Questions and answers	Homophones
	Dear Dad (870L)	Questions and answers	Working out meanings fr context; new words
Family	**Lesson**	**Reading Comprehension**	**Vocabulary**
	Brother and Sister	Questions and answers	Unscrambling words
	A Martian Homecoming (1050L)	Questions and answers	Colour words
History	**Lesson**	**Reading Comprehension**	**Vocabulary**
	The Date for Reform (1010L)	Questions and answers	Idioms about time
	Rajyasri and Her Brothers (660L)	Questions and answers	Words used to describe p
	Ozymandias	Questions and answers	Antonyms; using a diction
	The Sea	Questions and answers	Collective nouns
Words	**Lesson**	**Reading Comprehension**	**Vocabulary**
	Why Books are Dangerous (1020L)	Questions and answers	New words about telling s
	Horsemail (1110L)	Questions and answers	New words about communication
	Pretty Words	Questions and answers	Similes
Science	**Lesson**	**Reading Comprehension**	**Vocabulary**
	When the Martians Landed (740L)	Questions and answers	Words which take on diffe parts of speech
	Elevators and Escalators	Questions and answers	Alliteration
	Science Star Omar (940L)	Questions and answers	Matching words and mear
Nature	**Lesson**	**Reading Comprehension**	**Vocabulary**
	The Caged Thrush Freed and Home Again	Questions and answers	Prefixes
	The Man Who Wanted to Fly	Questions and answers	Synonyms
	Life Before the Dinosaurs (860L)	Questions and answers Marking true or false	Making shorter words fro longer ones Suffixes
Sports	**Lesson**	**Reading Comprehension**	**Vocabulary**
	The Trial (570L)	Questions and answers	Metaphors about sports
	The Spirit of Cricket (1350L)	Questions and answers	Word meanings

rammar	Writing	Making connections between lessons Class discussion Listening and remembering
ountable and uncountable nouns	Dividing writing into paragraphs	
uantifiers	Informal letter	
rammar	Writing	Discussion of the theme Making connections Debate on nuclear vs joint families Making a family tree
omparative adjectives; noun as djective	Discussion of the idea that literature should have a moral	
rammar	Writing	Making connections Reciting and listening to poetry Independent research about authors
dverbs	Writing a character sketch	
ast perfect tense		
rammar	Writing	Debate on books and their impact Debate on letters vs emails Listening to poetry and recognising similes Independent research
ast continuous tense	Writing a book review	
uture perfect tense	Writing a short story	
rammar	Writing	Discussion about intelligent life in the universe. Discussion about the merits of technology. Independent research Report on a book or movie
ctive and passive voice	Writing a descriptive paragraph	
onjunctions	Researching and writing about a famous person	
rammar	Writing	Recognising a type of poem Making connections Independent research Making a speech
ronouns	Writing a diary entry	
ossessive, reflexive and reciprocal ronouns		
Grammar	Writing	Making connections Discussion about the influence of television Listening and making note of important points
Clauses	Paragraph writing	
Noun clauses		

Introduction

Advanced English is a series of course books, workbooks and literature readers for students of classes 6, 7 and 8. The books are based on the current NCERT curriculum. The series uses a communicative approach to help students improve their written and verbal skills, and to inculcate a deeper appreciation of the English language.
In addition, the books aim to foster a love of literature and reading in children.
Advanced English has been designed to cover the essential skills of the language:

Language development
- Reading comprehension
- Vocabulary
- Grammar

Communication skills
- Writing
- Activities
- Listening

Social and other skills
- Debate
- Independent research
- Speaking

Some of the unique features of the series are:

Lexile measures
The Lexile framework for reading was created by MetaMetrics, the educational research organisation. Lexile measures assess the difficulty level of a piece of writing. *Advanced English* course books and supplementary readers have been lexiled by MetaMetrics. All the texts in these books are within or slightly above the recommended range of lexile scores for that age group. This means that the texts are of a level accessible to the students, yet still challenging. The average range of lexile scores for a student of class six is 665–1000L.

Continuous and Comprehensive Evaluation
The CBSE describes CCE as a "system of school-based assessment that covers all aspects of student's development. It emphasizes two-fold

objectives: continuity in evaluation and assessment of broad-based learning." The CBSE recommends the implementation of CCE after class nine, but the principle of broad-based learning is one that we believe should be implemented throughout the school career. A table at the back of the book allows teachers to evaluate the student's progress on a number of parameters at regular intervals throughout the year.

Selection of texts

The course book features a diverse selection of works by major Indian and international authors. There are stories, poems, plays, speeches and articles that are diverse in both genre and style.

Themed sections

The lessons are divided by theme, based on NCERT recommendations. Each theme features a relevant quote and a page for further exploring the links between the lessons and the theme. The book aims to encourage the students to make connections across chapters, and to identify and discuss broader issues. To this end, the theme pages also include further discussion, listening and speaking exercises in which the students are given debate topics and ideas to discuss.

Encouragement of independent thought and expression

Advanced English encourages students to form and defend opinions. The reading comprehension and further discussion sections contain a number of open-ended questions to which there is no definitive right or wrong answer. The listening and speaking exercises also encourage debate and active participation in the classroom. A variety of creative writing exercises give the students further practice in expressing their thoughts with originality and clarity.

Acquiring tools for independent learning

Through the learn more and activities sections, the students are encouraged to research specific subjects by themselves. The theme-based approach further enhances critical thinking skills, while a number of vocabulary exercises call for the use of the dictionary or thesaurus.

Attractive, "grown-up" format
The unusual size and layout of the book signify the students' transition from primary to middle school. The inclusion of high-quality black-and-white artwork further enhances the appeal of the book, making the reading experience more enjoyable.

Rigorous and challenging exercises
The vocabulary and grammar sections are accompanied by practice exercises. Further practice exercises can be found in the workbook.

Art and literature have always shared a symbiotic relationship. Such a cross-pollination of genres not only enriches the former, but informs the latter. Many visual learners will find that these connections allow for better retention of the material and enable an engagement that is above mere rote-learning. It is for this reason that we chose to use cover images based on the work of some of the world's great artists.

The cover of this book is based on the *Portrait of Adele Bloch-Bauer I*, by Gustav Klimt. Klimt was a Symbolist painter from Austria. He was the son of a gold engraver, and a number of his paintings, including this one, make use of gold leaf. In 2006 the *Portrait of Adele Bloch-Bauer I* was sold for 135 million US dollars, making it, at the time, the most expensive painting ever sold.

GROWING UP

"We grow neither better nor worse as we get old,
but more like ourselves."

— May Lamberton Becker

1 In the Playground

Nury Vittachi is an author and journalist from Sri Lanka. He is best known for his series of comedy crime books, The Feng Shui Detective. *This chapter is taken from* Twilight in the Land of Nowhen.

The bell rang.

Rivers of children poured out of the classrooms and a **deluge** of **scampering** legs spilled down the stairs to the **bleak** playground where Simon was sitting.

He hated playtime slightly less than class. During class he was always in **grave** danger of humiliation. The teacher could point to him and ask him to speak at any time. And opening his mouth always led to **misery**. Whatever he said was out of step with everyone else.

But during playtime, he didn't need to talk to anyone. He could just sit in a corner by himself. People would just think that he was one of those kids who

---

deluge: a great quantity of something arriving at the same time
scampering: running with quick, light steps, especially through fear or excitement
bleak: dreary
grave: solemn, serious
misery: wretched unhappiness or discomfort

liked to sit by themselves in a miserable, **hostile** way. Which suited him just fine.

He had found a quiet spot on a **battered** green bench, one of a line of old benches running down one side of the playground. A few other shy kids sat there, including a girl with red hair and glasses, and a couple of kids whose main language was Korean.

For several minutes, he sat there and watched children in the playground running and shouting and talking and pushing each other around.

No one paid any attention to him and he started to relax for the first time that day.

Time passed.

He sat.

He watched.

Time passed.

He would have got through that first break time just fine, but for Trudie Stig. She was the sort of person Simon most hated, the sort of person he always avoided. Sadly for him, there seemed to be people all over the place who had the same, sickening quality that she had: Friendliness.

He grunted and nodded in a distinctly unfriendly way as she approached. Two other girls followed. They were loud and pretty and ultra-confident in a scary way: the sort of girls who looked too perfect, like pictures on the covers of glossy magazines. He focussed on his feet.

"Hi," she said.

Without looking up, he mumbled: "Simon."

"You're the new boy, aren't you? What's your name?"

He sighed. This was going to be difficult. "Art."

The three girls looked at each other. Two of them giggled.

"Really?" said Trudie, still trying to be friendly. "Like short for Arthur? What's your favourite lesson?"

"Easterpark."

---

hostile: antagonistic, opposed
battered: damaged by age and repeated use

The three girls flashed their eyes at each other again.

The one with blond ringlets put her hand to her mouth and laughed. "That's a place, not a lesson, Dorkbrain," she sneered. "You're from around here? Which part?"

"I hate this school," he said.

The blond girl made a "he's-crazy-so-let's-get-out-of-here" sign by spinning her index finger at the side of her head. She whispered to the girl next to her: "His name's Poopoo."

But Trudie, who had brown hair and brown eyes and was the most beautiful girl he had ever seen, was still trying to be friendly.

"Is something wrong?" she asked.

"So are you," he snapped at her friend.

Eliza grabbed her arm and pulled her away. She turned her head and shouted at him: "Bye, weirdo!" The three girls ran off laughing.

Yep. Exactly as he had expected. Life at this school was going to be the same as it had been at all the others: a disaster.

Reading Comprehension

1 Answer the following questions.

i Did Simon prefer playtime to class? Why?

ii What helped Simon to relax at the playground?

iii What "sickening" quality did Trudie Stig have?

iv Why do you think Simon "nodded in an unfriendly way"?

v Read the conversation between Simon and the girls. Why do you think the other students found it difficult to understand him?

vi Who were the other children sitting on the old benches? Why do you think they were there?

vii What kind of person was Trudie Stig? Describe her.

Vocabulary

Reporting words

Words like **say** and **said** are neutral words. They do not tell us how (in what manner) someone said something. They can be replaced by **reporting words** that describe different ways of speaking, like mumbled, screamed, shouted, etc.

1 Underline the word that describes how something was said. The first has been done for you.

i Without looking up, he <u>mumbled</u>: "Simon."

ii She whispered to the girl next to her: "His name's Poopoo."

iii "Is something wrong?" she asked.

iv "So are you," he snapped at her friend.

v The maths teacher explained the formula to us.

vi "Get out of my sight!" shouted the angry policeman.

2 Choose words from the box to complete the following sentences.

cried	whispered	yelled	warned
screamed	asked	stuttered	laughed

i My mother ________________ us that we were getting late.

ii "That was a good joke!" ________________ Aruna.

iii He ________________ out in pain when the doctor touched the injured foot.

iv After the play, we ________________ the lead actor for his autograph.

v "I've got a secret," ____________ Shikha.

vi "It's a g-g-g-ghost!" ____________ Bill.

vii "There's a snake in the garden!" ____________ Lavanya.

viii The coach ____________ out instructions from the sidelines.

Grammar

Nouns: Countable Nouns

Nouns are words which refer to things, people, places or feelings.
Countable nouns are nouns which can be described with numbers.
For example: **Cup** is a countable noun, whereas **rice** is an uncountable noun. We can talk of **five cups**, but it is not possible to speak of **five rice**. To describe the amount of rice we would have to use words like **some** or **more**.

1 Classify the following into countable and uncountable nouns.

sand	pig	mountain	water
lake	carrot	anger	milk
lamp	crayon	air	tree
music	butter	tractor	dinosaur
warmth	tea	poster	stapler
bottle	metal	keyboard	trampoline
flour			

Countable Nouns	Uncountable Nouns
pig	sand

Writing

Paragraph

A **paragraph** is a section within a story or article which deals with a single idea or event. The text is divided into paragraphs in order to make it easier for the reader to understand.

1 Read the chapter and note how the paragraphs are separated. Now, divide the piece given here into paragraphs.

He was in a classroom. He knew no one. No one knew him. He looked around. From his point of view, the classroom was crawling with revolting, dribbling, shouting brats. There were thirty-two of them. They all looked exactly like the kids in all the other schools he had been to: kids who didn't become his friends; kids who became dangerous, lifelong enemies. They were that much older than they had been at his six previous schools, just as he was that much older. Each time, they were larger. Each time, the nightmare was worse. The noise of squalling, gossiping children was deafening. The room smelt of disinfectant. The strip-lights above them were flickering on and off. The paint on the walls was grey and old. Bits of it were peeling off. There was no one there who knew about his problem. This was going to be horrible. He could feel it in his bones. It was going to be hideous beyond words. It was going to be tragic.

2 The Schoolboy

***William Blake** (1759–1827) was a famous English poet and artist. Blake was from a middle-class family and never went to school. He was later known for his revolutionary politics. This poem is from his* Songs of Innocence.

I love to rise in a summer morn,
When the birds sing on every tree;
The distant huntsman winds his horn,
And the skylark sings with me:
O what sweet company!

But to go to school in a summer morn,—
O it drives all joy away!
Under a **cruel** eye outworn,
The little ones spend the day
In **sighing** and **dismay**.

Ah then at times I **drooping** sit,
And spend many an **anxious** hour;
Nor in my book can I take delight,
Nor sit in learning's **bower**,
Worn through with the dreary shower.

How can the bird that is born for joy
Sit in a cage and sing?
How can a child, when fears annoy,
But droop his tender wing,
And forget his youthful spring!

O father and mother if buds are **nipped**,
And blossoms blown away;

cruel: causing pain or suffering
sighing: emitting a long, deep, audible exhalation, expressing sadness, tiredness, relief, etc.
dismay: consternation and distress
drooping: bending or hanging downwards limply
anxious: experiencing worry or unease
bower: a pleasant shady place under trees, a summerhouse or shaded enclosure
nipped: remove something by pinching or squeezing sharply

And if the tender plants are stripped
Of their joy in the springing day,
By sorrow and care's dismay,—

How shall the summer arise in joy,
Or the summer fruits appear?
Or how shall we gather what griefs destroy,
Or bless the **mellowing** year,
When the blasts of winter appear?

Reading Comprehension

1 Answer the following questions.

i Whose do you think is the "cruel eye"?

ii Is the speaker against education and acquiring knowledge?

iii In the fourth stanza, the schoolboy compares himself to a bird. How? What does he mean by "droop his tender wing"?

iv To whom is the poem addressed?

v In what way is the child comparable to a "tender plant"? What do you think the poet is referring to when he speaks of "summer fruits" and "the blasts of winter"?

vi Do you agree with this poem?

Vocabulary

Homophones

Homophones are words which sound the same but have different meanings.

1 In the following sentences, circle the correct word from the brackets.

i (I/Eye) wish we didn't have to go to school.

---

mellowing: softened by maturity

ii When the huntsman blew his horn he scared off his (pray/ prey).

iii The small grey donkey (braid/brayed) loudly as I walked past.

iv When the boy grew up he became a great (naval/navel) captain.

v To make bread you must (need/knead) the (dough/doe).

vi The (creek/creak) of the old chair when I sit down distracts me.

vii My dog barks whenever he (sees/seize) the postman.

viii We (pride/pried) the lid off the box and looked inside.

ix My mother applied (coal/kohl) to her eyes before going out.

x In art class we mix our paints on a (palette/pallet).

3 Dear Dad

***Paro Anand** has written a number of books for children and has performed her stories in various parts of India and Europe. This piece is from her collection of short stories,* School Ahead!

Dear Dad,

No MON,

No FUN,

Your son

Dear Son,

Too bad,

So sad,

Your Dad

Dear Mum,

I have a feeling you didn't see my telegram, because you are so sensitive, so understanding and so generous. If you had seen my **desperate** telegram, you would definitely have done something about it. So my darling, darling mother, I'm sure that you cannot see your little chick who has just flown the coop, suffer the problems of economic **constraints**.

Your loving son

Dear Son,

Pockets empty, I'm very senti, but very broke, it's no joke so ask your da,

Your loving Ma

---

desperate: feeling, showing or involving despair
constraints: limitation or restriction

(sigh) Dear Dad,

Got Ma's reply to my letter. I am very disturbed to know that she is feeling financially tight. In this day and age of gender equality, it disturbs me that my own mother has no control over the family purse strings.

Your loving son

Dear son,

Ma gets pocket money, so do you. I want you to make it on your own. So buckle down to tightening your own purse strings just like the rest of us are doing.

Your father

Huh, can't even end with "your loving father". I know he's my father, what I need to know is, whether he's my loving father or not. You see, they've sent me away. To boarding school, boreding school more like. A school so far away from civilisation, it might as well be on the moon. Where you have to wake up at 4.30 a.m. when it's fully dark and shivery. They make you exercise on empty stomachs, run around the field, do deep breathing when you'd really rather be deep sleeping and then feed you hot porridge with lumps, that, I suppose are also put there "for your own good".

Now there's our monthly day out approaching. But, as you probably know by now, I'm rather financially challenged.

I'm not going. Sadly I announce to my so-called friends that I will not go on the monthly **outing** to civilisation because of bankruptcy. I

---

outing: a short trip taken for pleasure

was hoping that they'd want my **cheery** company so badly that they would offer to pay for me. They were completely **heartless** and shrugged and continued making their plans for the outing.

There was nothing I could do except to feel completely sorry for myself. Actually, it just occurred to me that there was something better. I could make my parents feel really guilty. Yes, that would cheer me up a little ...

---

cheery: happy and optimistic

heartless: completely lacking in feeling or consideration

My dear, dear parents,

I hope this letter finds you in the very best of health and spirits. I do hope it does because I'm hoping that you have enough good health and spirits for me as well. I myself am very low. I have lost a lot of weight. I have lost muscle tone and hair and my skin is **sallow** and pale too. This is because the food here is not as good as your cooking, dear mother! (Aside to self—ha! ha! Cooking? My mother couldn't make tea if her life depended on it.)

Even as I write this epistle, all my friends have gone to the nearby town. There is a wonderful film that the teacher recommended we see, as it is full of value education. Unfortunately, I did not have any money, as you refused to send me any. I do hope that this has been a mere oversight. I therefore, humbly request you to dispatch some desperately needed cash forthwith so that I am not shamed and embarrassed like this in the future.

I sincerely hope that this letter finds you in the best of health and spirits.

I remain (what choice do I have but to remain so?),

Your loving son ...

Epilogue

Well, my parents never did send me extra cash. They did write, but there were nothing but kind words in it for me. When they came to collect me at the end of term, they commented that I had not lost much weight at all. I couldn't argue too much about that because my report card left me in no position to make further demands. Maybe next time I'll do brilliantly and then be able to demand a better financial status. But then again, maybe nothing will change at all.

sallow: (of a person's face or complexion) of a yellowish or pale colour

epilogue: a section or speech at the end of the book serving as a comment on or conclusion to what has happened

Reading Comprehension

1 Answer the following questions.

- i Why does the narrator write to his mother instead of his father?
- ii How do the narrator's friends react when they learn that he cannot join them for the outing? How did he hope they would react?
- iii What advice does the narrator's father give him?
- iv "...hot porridge with lumps, that, I suppose are also put there 'for your own good.'" Do you think the narrator means this seriously?
- v What makes the narrator feel better?
- vi Why couldn't he argue with his parents at the end of term?
- vii Do you think that the narrator's parents are strict? Why or why not?
- viii Compare the narrator's first letter to his last. What differences do you notice in the style? Why do you think this has happened?

Vocabulary

1 What do the following phrases mean? Try to work out the meanings from the context in which they are used.

- i financially challenged
- ii tightening your own purse strings
- iii very broke
- iv buckle down

2 Of the words in the box, only three are not connected to letters and letter writing. Can you circle these words?

missive	epistle	billet
enchilada	memorandum	telegram
concurrence	message	milliner
postcard	note	reply
email	correspondence	post

Grammar

Quantifiers

Quantifiers are words that come before nouns, by telling us **how many** or **how much**. The quantifiers we can use for a noun depend on whether the noun is countable or uncountable.

Quantifiers for uncountable nouns include the following: much, not much, a little, very, little, a bit of, a good deal of.

Quantifiers for countable nouns include: many, a few, few, several, a couple of, none of.

Quantifiers that can be used for both include: all of the, some, most of, plenty of, lack of, enough, a lot of.

1 Find out where the quantifiers have been used incorrectly and substitute them with the correct quantifier.

i a bit of rabbits ____________________

ii a few bricks ____________________

iii many rice ____________________

iv some pirates ____________________

v a lot of books ______________________

vi a great deal of people ______________________

vii a couple of light ______________________

viii several gardens ______________________

ix none of the water ______________________

x a lack of doorbells ______________________

xi too much stones ______________________

xii a little giraffes ______________________

xiii too many milk ______________________

xiv too many cooks ______________________

xv a couple of salt ______________________

xvi plenty of examples ______________________

Writing

Imagine you are at boarding school and have forgotten to bring your coat. Write an informal letter to your parents asking them to send it to you. Remember to include your address and the date in the top left or right corner of the page.

Further Discussion

1 What do you notice about the setting (where the story takes place) of the three chapters in this section?

2 In *Twilight in the Land of Nowhen*, Simon does not want to make friends. In *Dear Dad*, the narrator is disappointed with his "so-called friends". Discuss these two characters. Which of them do you feel sympathy for, and why?

Listening and Speaking

Discuss in class what you think are the most important things about growing up. Some of these could be:

- i being able to vote.
- ii being able to drive.
- iii going to college.

Your class teacher will write down your suggestions and read out the list. Try to remember as many items as you can from the list and write them down. See how many you remember!

FAMILY

"Call it a clan, call it a network, call it a tribe, call it a family. Whatever you call it, whoever you are, you need one."

—Jane Howard

4 Brother and Sister

***Lewis Carroll** (1832–98) was an English writer and mathematician. His real name was Charles Lutwidge Dodgson. He is most famous for having written* Alice's Adventures in Wonderland.

"SISTER, sister, go to bed!
Go and rest your **weary** head."
Thus the **prudent** brother said.

"Do you want a battered hide,
Or scratches to your face
applied?"
Thus his sister calm replied.

"Sister, do not raise my **wrath**.
I'd make you into mutton **broth**
As easily as kill a moth."

The sister raised her **beaming**
eye
And looked on him **indignantly**
And sternly answered, "Only
try!"

Off to the cook he quickly ran.
"Dear Cook, please lend a frying pan
To me as quickly as you can."

"And wherefore should I lend it you?"
"The reason, Cook, is plain to view.
I wish to make an Irish **stew**."

---

weary: tired
prudent: wise
wrath: extreme anger
broth: a thin soup of meat or vegetable stock, sometimes thickened with barley or other cereals

beaming: radiant
indignantly: with annoyance
stew: cook slowly in liquid in a closed dish

"What meat is in that stew to go?"
"My sister'll be the contents!"
"Oh"
"You'll lend the pan to me, Cook?"
"No!"

Moral: Never stew your sister.

Reading Comprehension

1 Answer the following questions.

i Do you think that the brother is "prudent" or the sister "calm"? Why does the poet use these words to describe them?

ii Why do you think the sister threatens her brother in the second stanza?

iii What does the brother threaten to do to his sister?

iv "My sister'll be the contents!"/"Oh". Do you think the Cook's reaction is funny or unexpected? Why?

v Why is there a "moral" at the end of the poem? What do you think of the moral "Never stew your sister"?

Vocabulary

1 Unscramble the letters to find words that are related to cooking. The first one has been done for you.

i	mimers	simmer
ii	lobi	__________
iii	yringf	__________
iv	ikngba	__________
v	capsanue	__________

vi rilgl ____________________

vii cromaview ____________________

viii tetkle ____________________

ix supersre-crooke ____________________

x kennidag ____________________

Discussion

The poem "Brother and Sister" ends with a very strange moral. Do you think all stories and poems should have a moral? Why?

5 A Martian Homecoming

***Vandana Singh** is a physics instructor and a science fiction writer. Her best-known children's books are the* Younguncle *books*—Younguncle Comes to Town *and* Younguncle in the Himalayas.

Here Amrita was at last, standing with a group of people, on Mars itself. Mars City had so far been a confusing **blur**. Two days had not been enough to get used to the fact that most of Mars City was underground. She had seen holo-films of Mars City many times on the spaceship, but they had not prepared her for the reality: the peculiar feeling of lightness, the pinkish-yellow sky and the great, arid desert, coloured in shades of brown and yellow, orange and red. And the fine yellow dust that seemed to get in everywhere. And having to wear a walksuit outside the **domes** of Mars City, because the air of Mars was too thin and unbreathable, and because the walksuit protected her from dangerous **cosmic radiation**. The days on Mars were called sols, not days, and were slightly longer than on Earth. And Mars had two little, **misshapen** moons, instead of one big one.

The officials from Mars City had finally yielded to her insistence that she be allowed to come with them in their big all-terrain vehicle with the medical supplies and emergency personnel. Olympus Mons rose in front of her, so high that she could not see the top, only the endless slope, and far, far above, the beginning of the great cliff-face. They were on the lower slopes of the mountain. She, Amrita, standing on the highest mountain in the solar system!

For a moment she understood the wildness that was in her father, the urge to discover and explore, to see fantastic new **vistas**. She realised for the first time that there was something of that in her as well. She took a deep breath to calm herself. The ground below her feet was hard and cold, but her walksuit kept her warm. The day was

---

blur: indistinct and hazy in outline or appearance; obscure
dome: a rounded vault forming the roof of a building or structure
cosmic: of or relating to the universe or cosmos
radiation: action or process of radiating
misshapen: not having the normal or natural shape
vista: a view

fairly clear for Mars, with only a light dust haze, and the yellow sun shone small and valiant in the pink-and-butterscotch sky.

"It was a malfunction in the robot mobile unit," one of the officials had told her. "Your father had an accident that damaged the communications system, and he himself was injured—not much," he added quickly. "But he couldn't contact us and he was all alone up there, trying to repair the RMU. We flew by several times but he was in a **cleft** between two cliffs, and we didn't see him."

And now he was coming back. He had insisted on staying up there for three sols and working on repairs instead of returning tamely with the rescue craft that had found him. He had wanted to leap off Olympus Mons as he had planned, and now his daughter would see him do it.

After what seemed like the longest time, she thought she saw a dot high up in the air, near the rise of the cliffs. It came **arcing** through the air toward them, getting bigger and bigger, until she could make out

cleft: a fissure or split in a rock or the ground

arcing: move with a curving trajectory

the wings of the craft like two great sails, and the tiny cabin suspended between them. People around her cheered and the news reporters' robot cameras rose up in the air and flashed.

But Amrita had eyes only for her father, as the robot mobile unit swooped low over the ground. She saw the wheels emerge, hit the ground, the sails fan out, a flash of fire from the front **nozzle** of the craft, and then it was still, with the emergency people running toward it. She pushed anxiously forward and then saw, through her tears, her father's helmeted face and his triumphant wave.

She was home.

Reading Comprehension

1 Answer the following questions.

- i Where was Amrita?
- ii Why did she have to wear a walksuit?
- iii In what ways was Mars different to Earth?
- iv What is Olympus Mons?
- v What trait did Amrita and her father have in common?
- vi What do you think was Amrita's father's profession?
- vii Why had Amrita's father gone missing?
- viii Do you think the last line is important? Why?

Vocabulary

One thing that Amrita notices about Mars is the "pinkish-yellow sky". The colours on Mars are very different from those on Earth. Read the text and find more instances where she notices the unusual colours.

nozzle: a spout at the end of a pipe, hose or tube used to control a jet of liquid or gas

1 Five of the words in the box below are not the names of colours. Can you identify them?

ochre	entropy	cerulean	fuchsia
panjandrum	burgundy	cerise	foliage
azure	sienna	dugong	teal
chartreuse	cyan	aquamarine	volatile

Grammar

Comparative Adjectives

Adjectives are words that tell us more about nouns. They can be used before a noun.

Comparative adjectives are used when we want to compare a noun to something else. ***For example***, in comparing the length of two trees we say one is **taller** than the other.

This can be done by adding **er** to the end of the word (longer, taller, softer, etc.).

When a word ends with **e**, we can just add an **r** to it (larger, wiser, etc.).

In the case of words ending with **y**, we remove the **y** and add **ier** (heavier, earlier, etc.).

For some adjectives, we add the words **more** or **less** (more powerful, less intelligent).

The following adjectives have irregular forms:

Adjective	**Comparative Adjective**
good	better
well	better
bad	worse
far	further/farther
little	less
many	more

1 Fill in the blanks using the comparative form of the adjectives in the brackets.

i Sumit is ______________ than Karan. (strong)

ii Russia is ______________ than France. (big)

iii Mahek is tall. But Anjana is ______________. (tall)

iv Brown bread is ______________ for your health than white bread. (good)

v Harini is jealous because my project is ______________ than hers. (difficult)

vi That motorbike has a ______________ engine than mine. (powerful)

vii My brother Rohan is ______________ than my cousin Feroz. (strong)

viii When Aarushi tore the magazine, the librarian looked ______________ than we had ever seen her look. (angry)

ix After I realised I'd forgotten my homework, my day went from bad to ______________. (bad)

x Yoginder was ______________ than the average boy. (smart)

Nouns as Adjectives

A noun is a word that refers to a person, place or thing, while an adjective describes a noun. However, sometimes a noun is used to describe another noun. In these cases, a noun is filling the role of an adjective.

For example: Ritesh is a **car** salesman.

The word **car** is a noun, since it refers to a thing. But here, the word is used to describe the *type* of salesman (salesman is also a noun, since it refers to a person).

2 Underline the nouns which have been used to describe other nouns.

i Spot refused to eat dog food.

ii I would like a chicken sandwich.

iii My mother likes to read detective novels, but my sister prefers love stories.

iv Deepak was afraid of the street dogs.

v Where is Kirti's silk scarf?

vi Jasmine filled the empty jam jar with water and arranged the flowers in it.

3 Fill in the blanks with words from the box. The first one has been done for you.

paper	art	chocolate	government
pencil	race	tomato	plastic
cotton			

i Mr Menon served us some delicious <u>tomato</u> soup.

ii They offered her a slice of the ______________ cake that Mr Menon had baked.

iii Every student must bring her own ______________ box.

iv Chitra used a ______________ towel to wipe her nose.

v The fruit-seller put the apples in a ______________ bag.

vi Sushila worked in a ______________ hospital.

vii We met Mr R. Narasimhan at an ______________ exhibition.

viii My uncle breeds ______________ horses in his stable.

Further Discussion

1 How do the brother and sister feel about each other in the poem? How does Amrita feel about her father? Compare the two chapters and how the characters feel about their families.

2 What do you imagine when you hear the word family? Do you think either of the families in this section is unusual? Why?

Listening and Speaking

A nuclear family is a small family consisting of parents and children who all live in the same place. A joint family is a bigger family, with grandparents, aunts, uncles and cousins living in the same place. Until quite recently, most Indian families were joint ones. Do you live in a nuclear or joint family? Organise a debate on the merits and demerits of both types of families.

Activity

Make a family tree at home, containing as many of your relatives as you know. You could ask the adults in your home for help. Or you could make a "family tree" made up of all your friends instead.

HISTORY

"History is a race between education and catastrophe."
—H.G. Wells

6 The Date for Reform

***Toby Brown** is a British author. He is best known for his books in the* Dead Famous *series. The following chapter is an extract from the book* Julius Caesar and his Foul Friends.

After this, Julius Caesar got down to business. The senate (in recognition of the fact that JC was the only man around capable of running the government) appointed him **dictator** for ten years. Now JC could turn his attention to the reforms that Rome desperately needed.

The trouble with Rome was that it was still run as a city. That was fine, for a city, but by 46 BC Rome wasn't just the city of Rome. It was most of the rest of the known world as well. JC himself had added Gaul and most of Spain to Roman territory. It was no good conquering all these lands and trying to run them using the same old government. So JC began a sweeping programme of reforms, at least one of which we still enjoy today...

i JC increased the number of **senators** from 600 to 900 (allowing foreigners and soldiers in for the first time).

ii To prevent slave **uprisings** and to ensure that poor citizens could find work, JC made it law that one in three men working the land had to be free (that is, not slaves).

---

dictator: a ruler with total power over a country, an autocrat
senators: members of a senate
uprisings: acts of resistance or rebellions

iii JC settled his **veterans** on good land; some in Italy, some in Gaul and some in Africa.

iv In an attempt to **restrain** Rome's **extravagant** waste, JC banned certain luxury goods.

While pushing through these reforms, JC also pardoned many of the men who'd fought against him in the civil war. Men like Cassius Longinus and Marcus Brutus were even given jobs in JC's government, despite having been followers of Pompey before.

Next JC turned his attention to the Roman calendar.

Rome's calendar used twelve months based on the cycle of the moon. Priests put in extra days to keep it in step with the seasons. Sometimes they forgot, with **dire consequences**.

Instead of having weeks, the Romans divided their months into the calends (the 1st), the nones (the 7th) and the ides (the 15th). Other days were known by where they sat in relation to these markers.

In Alexandria JC had met an astronomer called Sosigenes. He'd worked out a calendar that was based on the sun instead of the moon.

Each year in the new calendar was to have 365 days, except every fourth year which would have an extra day (sounds familiar?). The year would begin on the first of January and each month would switch between thirty-one and thirty days long, except February which JC said should have twenty-nine days normally and thirty days in a leap year. In recognition of JC's contribution (and as a way of voting him

---

veterans: persons who have had long experience in a particular field
restrain: prevent from doing something
extravagant: lacking restraint in spending money or using resources
dire: extremely serious
consequences: results

even more honours) the senate named the month of July after him. (This led to a bit of confusion later when Emperor Augustus decided to name a month after himself. Augustus stole a day from February and added it to August so that his month wouldn't be shorter than JC's.)

Finally, to get the calendar back in step with the seasons, JC ordered an extra eighty days inserted into 46 BC, making it one of the longest years in history. JC called it "the last year of confusion".

Reading Comprehension

1 Answer the following questions.

i To what position was JC elected?

ii Why was Rome in need of reforms?

iii How did JC prevent slave uprisings? Why do you think this worked?

iv How did the Romans identify the days of the month?

v How many days were there in February according to Sosigenes' calendar? Why did this change?

vi What was "the last year of confusion"? Why was it so called?

2 Mark the following sentences true or false.

i The senate appointed JC dictator for life.

ii JC allowed foreigners and soldiers to become senators.

iii JC had all the men who had fought against him executed.

iv Sosigenes' calendar was based on the moon.

v The month of July is named after JC.

vi Cassius Longinus and Marcus Brutus were friends of JC.

vii JC made it easier for poor citizens to find work.

viii JC ignored his veterans.

Vocabulary

1 Find the definition closest in meaning to these idioms about time.

i	ahead of one's time	after a long wait
ii	after hours	struggling to complete something before a deadline
iii	at long last	after closing time; not during regular hours
iv	from time to time	to get a promise to avail of an offer at a later date
v	time is money	an idea which may not be fully understood until some later time in the future
vi	against the clock	occasionally
vii	to get a rain check	time is valuable

Grammar

Adverbs

Adverbs give us information about verbs, adjectives or other adverbs.

She walked **quickly** down the street.

Here the adverb **quickly** describes the verb **walked**.

Cinderella looked **extremely** pretty in her dress.

The adverb **extremely** tells us more about the adjective **pretty**.

She drives **incredibly slowly**.

The adverb **incredibly** tells us more about the adverb **slowly**, which describes the verb **drives**.

Types of Adverbs

Adverbs of manner usually describe **how** an action takes place. They often end in **ly**.
For example: quickly, slowly, angrily, happily, sleepily, fast, always, thoughtlessly, grumpily, hungrily.
Adverbs of time tell us when an action happened/will happen.
Come with me **now**.
We will meet **tomorrow**.
Adverbs of frequency describe how often an action takes place.
She is **always** late to work.
We **often** take the dog for a walk in the park.
Akhil **sometimes** works at his father's office after school.
Interrogative adverbs are usually placed at the beginning of a sentence and are used for asking questions about an action.
For Example: how, why, when, where.
Why are you here?
Who let the dogs out?

1 Choose adverbs from the box to complete the following sentences.

sweetly	angrily	fast	why
never	greedily	really	where
quietly	how		

i The school choir sang the Christmas carol ________________ .

ii ________________ can't you remember to close the gate when you come home?

iii Run ________________, or all the ice cream will be gone!

iv Tarun ________________ returns his library books on time.

v The children eyed the big cake ________________ .

vi "________________ have you left your pen?" shouted mother

________________ .

vii They spoke ________________ so that no one would hear them.

viii This new train moves ________________ fast.

ix ________________ have you been?

x "Look at those monkeys!" squealed Annu ________________.

7 Rajyasri and Her Brothers

***Devika Rangachari** has won a number of awards for her writings for children. Some of the books she has authored are* The Wit of Tenali Raman *and* The Merry Mischief of Gopal Bhand. *This chapter is exerpted from her book* Harsha Vardhana.

"And where do you think you're going?" snapped a **peremptory** voice. It was Vela, her mother's faithful nurse.

"I just wanted to see who had come," muttered Rajyasri sullenly. "I heard a horse and ..."

"That isn't any of your business," said the old lady grimly. "Your father has several hundred visitors in a day. Do you want to know the identity of each and every one? Perhaps you'd like to sit on the throne and help him run the kingdom?"

"I wish I could," flashed Rajyasri, her big eyes radiating **resentment**. "And I will some day. You just wait and see, Vela."

"You are already fourteen years old," sighed Vela. "When will you learn to behave like a proper princess? Always running around and poking your nose in your father's affairs! Even your mother wasn't like this at your age!"

"You're *her* nurse, not mine!" snapped Rajyasri and then, seeing the sudden hurt in the old lady's eyes, patted her hand **contritely**. "I'm sorry. I shouldn't have said that..." And she sidestepped neatly over to the inner courtyard where a group of boys were gossiping in a corner—her brothers Harsha and Rajya, and their cousin Bhandi.

Rajyasri didn't like Bhandi much. She nodded **curtly** at him and turned her attention to her brothers. The taller of the two **grasped** her hand and gently smoothed the curls away from her damp brow.

"You've been running," he remarked mildly.

"I was," and Rajyasri smiled at Rajya. He was very different from

---

peremptory: authoritative, not allowing for discussion
resentment: bitterness, indignation
contritely: expressing remorse
curtly: abruptly
grasped: seized and held firmly

the rest of them—quiet, gentle, soft-spoken and so **unassuming**.

"I suppose she heard the horse," remarked her other brother casually.

Harsha was tall and thin with long slender fingers that now drummed a rhythm on the carved wooden bench he was leaning against. He turned to smile at his sister.

It annoyed Rajyasri when he guessed correctly what she was thinking. It was difficult to conceal anything from him. Not like Rajya, Rajyasri thought wryly, who didn't have a single **conniving** bone in his

unassuming: not pretentious or arrogant

conniving: secretly allowing some wrongdoing, conspiring body and who wouldn't understand **guile** or **deceit** even if they stared him in the face.

"Our cousins have come," said Harsha. "They're from Malwa and their father's sent them here."

"But why?" demanded Rajyasri breathlessly.

"He lost a battle and wants to regroup his forces. So he's sent the two here out of harm's way."

"How do you know all this?" Rajya sounded mildly puzzled. "Did Father tell . . . ?"

"No, he didn't," interrupted Harsha. "But I make it my business to know things." He waved a hand in the direction of an approaching attendant. "And if I'm not mistaken, our father wants to see us now."

"Can I come too?" Rajyasri used her sweetest, most **coaxing** tone.

"You know you can't," said Harsha. "It's a matter of state, after all."

The easy tears sprang to Rajyasri's eyes. Rajya made a gesture of protest, but Harsha laughed and pulled one of her curls. "Don't you know when I'm teasing you?"

The princess blinked back her tears and gave the concerned Rajya a watery smile. Then she glared at Harsha's retreating figure. Sometimes she really hated him! She supposed she loved Harsha just as much as Rajya, but you never really knew where you were with him. Harsha could be warm and loving or cold and distant, all in the space of a few minutes. Unlike the predictable and **steadfast** Rajya.

Reading Comprehension

1 Answer the following questions.

- i Who was Rajyasri? Who was her father?
- ii What was the reason for Rajyasri's argument with Vela?
- iii Who were the visitors? Why had they come?
- iv Why was Rajyasri not expected to participate in state affairs?
- v What were Rajyasri's feelings towards her two brothers?

guile: sly or cunning intelligence
deceit: action or practice of deceiving
coaxing: persuading
steadfast: dutifully firm and unwavering

Vocabulary

The words in the crossword given here are all adjectives used to describe people in the story.

Across

1 imperious, insisting on obedience
4 sulky and bad-tempered
5 modest and unpretentious
7 persuasive
8 slim and graceful
9 apologetic, expressing remorse

Down

2 behaving in a way that is expected
3 plotting or conspiring
6 firm and unwavering

Grammar

Past Perfect Tense

The **past tense** is used to describe actions that happened in the past.

For example: We **sold** the car.

When we want to talk about something that happened *before* a particular point in the past, we use the **past perfect tense**.

For example: I **borrowed** money because I **had lost** my wallet.

Here, the action of borrowing money is in the past tense, but the action of losing the wallet happened *before* the money was borrowed.

1 Underline the verbs that are in the past perfect tense.

i I had never been abroad before my trip to Thailand.

ii Vivek missed the trip because he had forgotten his ticket.

iii My sister had been in Delhi for three years before she bought a house.

iv She had learnt both Sanskrit and German by the time she turned fifteen.

v My grandmother recalled how she and her sisters had grown sunflowers in the garden of their old house.

2 Fill in the blanks using the past perfect forms of the verbs given in the brackets.

i The rabbits ate all the vegetables that Suman __________ (plant) in the spring.

ii I __________ (never/eat) meat before I moved to Japan.

iii Kiran ate all the biryani that my brother __________ (cook).

iv By the time we reached, all the other guests ________________ (leave).

v We picked up all the cards that ________________ (fall) on the floor.

vi Revathy wore the sweater that she ________________ (knit) for herself.

Writing

Read how Rajyasri describes her two brothers in the story. Write a similar descriptive passage of a character in a book you have read. You could use some of the words given in the story.

8 Ozymandias

Percy Bysshe Shelley *(1792–1822) was one of the famous English Romantic poets. He was married to the novelist Mary Shelley.*

I met a traveller from an antique land
Who said: Two vast and trunkless legs of stone
Stand in the desert. Near them, on the sand,
Half sunk, a shattered visage lies, whose frown
And wrinkled lip, and sneer of cold command
Tell that its sculptor well those passions read
Which yet survive, stamped on these lifeless things,
The hand that mocked them and the heart that fed.
And on the pedestal these words appear:
"My name is Ozymandias, king of kings:
Look on my works, ye Mighty, and despair!"
Nothing beside remains. Round the decay
Of that colossal wreck, boundless and bare
The lone and level sands stretch far away.

Reading Comprehension

1 Answer the following questions.

  i What do you think is meant here by "an antique land"?

  ii What does the poem tell us about the statue? Can you describe it?

  iii What sort of person do you think the King was? Substantiate your answer with quotes from the poem.

  iv "Nothing beside remains." Why do you think the poet places this line here?

  v What do you think the poem is really about?

Vocabulary

Antonyms

An **antonym** is a word that means the opposite of a given word.

1 Reread the poem and find antonyms of the words given here.

  i modern ______________

  ii powerless ______________

  iii flourish ______________

  iv miniature ______________

  v hope ______________

2 Use your dictionary to find the meanings of the following words. See if you can use them in sentences of your own.

i visage ____________________

____

ii wreck ____________________

____

iii colossal ____________________

____

iv pedestal ____________________

____

v boundless ____________________

____

9 The Sea

George Gordon, Lord Byron *(1788–1824) was an English poet. He campaigned for social reform in the House of Lords and supported the Greek war of independence. This poem is an extract from his book* Childe Harold's Pilgrimage.

Roll on, thou deep and dark blue Ocean—roll!
Ten thousand fleets sweep over thee in vain;
Man marks the earth with ruin—his control
Stops with the shore;—upon the watery plain
The wrecks are all thy deed, nor doth remain
A shadow of man's ravage, save his own,
When for a moment, like a drop of rain,
He sinks into thy depths with bubbling groan,
Without a grave, unknelled, uncoffined, and unknown.

His steps are not upon thy paths,—thy fields
Are not a spoil for him,—thou dost arise
And shake him from thee; the **vile** strength he wields
For earth's destruction thou dost all despise,
Spurning him from thy **bosom** to the skies,
And send'st him, shivering in thy playful spray
And howling, to his gods, where haply lies
His **petty** hope in some near port or bay,
And dashest him again to earth:—there let him lay.

The **armaments** which thunderstrike the walls
Of rock-built cities, bidding nations quake,
And monarchs tremble in their capitals.
The oak **leviathans**, whose huge ribs make

---

vile: extremely unpleasant; morally bad, wicked
bosom: a woman's breast or chest; a person's loving care or protection
petty: trivial

armaments: military weapons and equipment
leviathans: something very large and powerful

Their clay creator the vain title take
Of lord of thee, and **arbiter** of war;
These are thy toys, and, as the snowy flake,
They melt into thy yeast of waves, which mar
Alike the Armada's pride, or spoils of Trafalgar.

Thy shores are empires, changed in all save thee —
Assyria, Greece, Rome, Carthage, what are they?
Thy waters washed them power while they were free
And many a **tyrant** since: their shores obey
The stranger, slave, or savage; their decay
Has dried up realms to deserts: not so thou,
Unchangeable save to thy wild waves' play —
Time writes no wrinkle on thine **azure** brow —
Such as creation's dawn beheld, thou rollest now.

arbiter: a person who settles a dispute
tyrant: cruel and oppressive ruler
azure: bright blue in colour

Reading Comprehension

1 Answer the following questions.

- i According to the poet, does Man control the sea?
- ii What are the "oak leviathans" referred to in the poem?
- iii What are the "toys" of the sea?
- iv Why does the poet refer to the Armada and Trafalgar? What were they?
- v The empires of Assyria, Greece, Rome and Carthage were once great, but unlike the sea they are no longer powerful. Which lines in the poem indicate this?
- vi What is the poem's attitude towards nature?

Vocabulary

Collective Nouns

Collective nouns are nouns we use to describe a group of objects (people, animals or things).

1 Match the objects listed here with their collective nouns.

	Object	Collective Noun
i	ships	cavalcade
ii	jewels	school
iii	dolphins	pod
iv	crows	cache
v	lorries	fleet
vi	horsemen	pack
vii	whales	murder
viii	cards	convoy

Further Discussion

1 Read these lines from "Ozymandias" and "The Sea".

"Look on my works, ye Mighty, and despair!"
Nothing beside remains. Round the decay
Of that colossal wreck, boundless and bare
The lone and level sands stretch far away."

"Thy waters washed them power while they were free
And many a tyrant since: their shores obey
The stranger, slave, or savage; their decay
Has dried up realms to deserts: not so thou,
Unchangeable save to thy wild waves' play—
Time writes no wrinkle on thine azure brow—"

What similarities do you see between these two poems? Do you think that the poets are trying to say the same thing?

2 Both the poems and "The Date for Reform" are related to the theme of time. Discuss.

Listening and Speaking

Listen to one of your classmates reading out the poem "The Sea" in class. What do you think makes it an effective poem? Is it beautiful? Why?

Learn More

The poets Byron and Shelley were close friends, along with a number of other famous poets of their time. Byron's daughter, Ada Lovelace, and Shelley's wife, Mary Shelley, are also famous. What is their claim to fame? Find out.

WORDS

"He ate and drank the precious Words,
his Spirit grew robust; He knew no more
that he was poor, nor that his frame was Dust."
—Emily Dickinson

10 Why Books Are Dangerous

***Neil Gaiman** is an English author of fantasy, comics and children's books. He lives in the USA.*

When I was a boy, I was almost always carrying a book. It might not have been obvious. Paperbacks were fairly easy to slip into pockets, after all. My father would **frisk** me for books before family weddings or funerals; otherwise he knew that, while other people were being bored, I'd be sitting comfortably, probably under a table, off in my own world, reading.

I liked books. I did not yet suspect that books were dangerous. I didn't care what the books were about, as long as they had a story of some kind—spy stories, horror stories, SF or fantasy, histories, adventures, tales. I'd read true-life stories about people who caught spies or captured rare animals for zoos or people who hunted down man-eating tigers. I was also very fond of detectives and the books they came in. These were,

---

frisk: pass the hands over someone to search for concealed items

I think, looking back on it, all very sensible things for a boy to like, and not the least bit dangerous.

The headmaster of my school in the south of England, a pipe-smoking, **gruff** gentleman, who was famous for his **precise** and painful use of the slipper on boys who were sent to him for misbehaving, once **confiscated** a book from me. It was called *And to my nephew Albert I leave the island what I won off up? Fatty Hagen in a poker game*, and it had a photograph of a naked lady on the cover, which was why it was confiscated. This seemed particularly unfair, as in the early 1970s, most books seemed to have naked ladies on the covers, which had little or nothing to do with what was going on inside the book. I was **interrogated** by the headmaster and was given the book back at the end of term, with a warning to watch what I read. He didn't use the slipper, though. Not that time.

Obviously the headmaster understood the dangers of books. He was trying to tell me something. I didn't listen.

Eventually I started to read the dangerous books.

The really dangerous books had titles like *1001 Jolly Interesting Things a Boy Can Do*. You could make dyes from common garden vegetables. It explained it all.

I read the article on making dyes from common garden vegetables, and then I boiled a beetroot and soaked a white school shirt in beet water, and turned it a purply sort of red. I decided that I wouldn't be caught dead wearing it. Then I put it in the washing, and it turned all the shirts and socks and underwear it was washed with a rather startling shade of pink.

I had not learned my lesson. The next thing I found was the toffee recipe.

I learned that if I melted some butter in a saucepan, and then added sugar and golden syrup and a tablespoon of water, and I heated it all together and got it very hot (but didn't burn it), and dripped drops of the boiling liquid into a glass of cold water, when the drops

---

gruff: abrupt or taciturn in manner
precise: exact, accurate

confiscated: take or seize with authority
interrogated: questioned

went solid, it was done. Then I'd pour it out onto a greased pie-pan, and let it set hard.

I was so proud. I'd made a golden-clear, buttery toffee. Pure sugar, with a little fat. It tasted amazing. Chewing it was a battle between the toffee and the teeth. This went on for several months.

I was in a math lesson. I'd put a fist-sized lump of the toffee into my pocket, where it had melted, slowly, to the shape of my leg. And I had forgotten about it. I also had a handkerchief in the pocket.

"You, boy," said the teacher. "Gaiman. You're **snivelling**, boy. Blow your nose."

I said, "Yes, sir," and pulled the handkerchief from the pocket. It came out, and as it did so, a large lump of toffee that was stuck to the handkerchief sailed out across and hit the tiled floor.

It shattered when it hit the floor, like glass, into several hundred sharp-edged fragments.

I spent the rest of the lesson on my knees, picking up the sticky-sharp bits of toffee from the floor, while the teacher, convinced that I had done this on purpose to be funny (as if I'd waste a huge lump of toffee on a joke), made **sarcastic** comments. And, at the end of the lesson, I was sent to the headmaster with a note explaining what I'd done.

The headmaster read the note, puffed on his pipe, then walked slowly to the cupboard at the back of his study and, opening it, produced a large slipper, and suggested that I might want to bend over.

That was the day I discovered that books were dangerous.

At least, books that suggested you do something ...

Reading Comprehension

1 Answer the following questions.

i What did the narrator's father do before family gatherings?

ii What sort of books did the narrator read?

iii What did the headmaster do to boys who misbehaved?

---

snivelling: sniffling

sarcastic: using irony or mockery to convey contempt

iv Which were the dangerous books? What made them dangerous?

v Had the narrator dropped the toffee in class as a joke? What makes you think so?

vi Do you think that books are dangerous?

Vocabulary

The words in the table are all related to different ways of telling stories. How many of them have you encountered?

poem	comic	epic
anecdote	tale	speech
joke	novel	essay
saga	narrative	recitation

Grammar

Past Continuous Tense

The **past continuous tense** is used to describe an action that happened in the past over a period of time.
For example: She **was driving** the car.
She **was drinking** her milk when the doorbell rang.
We can use words like **always** or **constantly** to show that a particular action happened repeatedly.
For example: Malini **was always quarreling** with her brother.
The past continuous tense can also be used to depict two actions happening simultaneously.
For example: While I **was listening** to music, my sister and her friends **were playing** cricket outside.

1 Fill in the blanks with the correct tense forms of the verbs in brackets.

i While Yamini __________ (sleep) the cat __________ (prowl) around the garden.

ii I __________ (clean) my room when my mother walked in.

iii What __________ you __________ (do) in there?

iv Sumit __________ (not work) hard enough to finish the job on time.

v While Hari __________ (run) away from the zombies,

Geetika __________ (search) for weapons.

vi Parvati __________ (always complain) about her parents.

vii Rachel __________ (wash) her car because it was dirty.

viii We __________ (wait) for Mohit and Almas.

ix The students __________ (play) football when the bell rang.

x Madhavi __________ (pull) Gayathri's hair.

Writing

1 What is the most important book you have ever read? Write a short review, telling the story in brief and explaining why it was good and how it influenced you.

2 The author describes a recipe for making toffee. Write out a recipe for any dish that you know how to cook. Give detailed instructions so that your reader finds it easy to follow.

11 Horsemail

***Siddhartha Sarma** is an Indian journalist and writer from Assam. He is best known for his book* The Grasshopper's Run.

There was a time when you wrote a letter on a piece of paper, sealed it in an envelope and dropped it in a red box (in India). From here it was picked up by somebody called a postman after which it was carried around the country to wherever you wanted it sent.

Much before that, in about 1860 in the US, there was no such system if you lived on the East Coast and had to send a letter to, say, Oregon on the West Coast.

The system began from Missouri to California, over 3,100 km, in 1860. Instead of sending mail on slow, **cumbersome** horse-drawn coaches, mailbags were loaded on individual riders. They would stop to change horses or transfer to other riders on the route at numerous stables specially set up for them.

It became an exercise in discovering how lightly you could travel on horseback. Quite soon, every extra bit of weight was removed till riders only had a bag of water and a revolver—both of which were needed, because this was in the days of the Old West. Services were round the clock, in every season. Some men even rode continuously for nearly a day, back and forth on relay.

The horsemen—and their horses—were, naturally, highly valued. Their pay was six times what an average labourer was paid then. These riders had such a reputation that even **outlaws** did not want to **ambush** them. It must have been a ride worth going on.

The Pony Express, as it came to be called, became **legendary**, proof of what man and horse could do, delivering letters and parcels from the Atlantic to the Pacific in ten days.

Eventually, the riders were outrun by the telegraph system and after more than a year of operation, the Pony Express was shut down.

But even today, the United States Postal Service uses the name as a trademark. And if you happen to be riding a horse and decide to see how fast you can go, for how long and want to make your pack weight lighter, you can, for a brief period, become a Pony Express rider. The internet, after all, does not bring the sound of the desert and mountain winds to your ears.

cumbersome: difficult, unwieldy
outlaws: fugitives from the law

ambush: a surprise attack by people lying in wait in a concealed position
legendary: very famous

Reading Comprehension

1 Answer the following questions.

i Why were mailbags sent on horses instead of coaches?

ii What essential items did the riders carry?

iii Why was the Pony Express shut down?

iv Why do you think the writer begins the piece with "there was a time"?

v "Eventually, the riders were outrun by the telegraph system". Comment on this statment.

Vocabulary

1 Which of the following words are *not* ways of sending messages that people have used over the years?

telegram	Pony Express	email
airmail	Morse code	platypus post
pigeon post	cardiogram	smoke signals

Grammar

Future Perfect Tense

We use the **future perfect tense** to describe an action that will already have been completed at some point in the future.

For example: By November I **will have finished repainting** the house.

Will she **have arrived** by seven o'clock?

The gardener **will have been working** here for twenty years next week.

1 Underline the verb in future perfect tense in the following sentences.

i By the time your sister joins school we both will have left.

ii Janaki will have completed the report by tomorrow.

iii Will she have heard the news?

iv In 2025 I will have lived in Delhi for twenty years.

v How many books are you going to have read by the end of the year?

2 Identify the tenses of the following sentences.

i Kriti was playing the guitar in her bedroom. ________________

ii He had written a long and indignant letter to the editor.

____

iii We could not attend the concert because Aparajita had forgotten to buy tickets. ________________

iv By the time the train arrived we had been waiting for four hours. ________________

v In June she will have entered class five. ________________

vi After the match we congratulated the team members.

____

vii We were going to the zoo when the car broke down.

____

viii I am going to have finished cooking by four o'clock.

____

Writing

Imagine you were a horseman delivering mail. Write a short story about your adventures.

12 Pretty Words

***Elinor Wylie** (1885–1928) was an American poet. In addition to poetry, she wrote eight novels and was the literary editor of* Vanity Fair *magazine for some time.*

Poets make pets of pretty, **docile** words:
I love smooth words, like gold-
enamelled fish
Which circle slowly with a silken swish,
And **tender** ones, like downy-feathered
birds:
Words shy and dappled, deep-eyed
deer in herds,
Come to my hand, and playful if I
wish,
Or purring softly at a silver dish,
Blue Persian kittens fed on cream
and curds.

I love bright words, words up and
singing early;
Words that are **luminous** in the dark,
and sing;
Warm lazy words, white cattle under
trees;
I love words **opalescent**, cool, and pearly,
Like midsummer moths, and honied words
like bees,
Gilded and sticky, with a little sting.

---

docile: submissive
enamelled: coated with an opaque or semitransparent glassy substance
tender: gentle

luminous: bright or shining
opalescent: showing many small points of shifting colour against a pale or dark ground
gilded: covered thinly in gold

Reading Comprehension

1 Answer the following questions.

i How does the poet describe "tender" words and "bright" words?

ii How many types of words does the poet describe here?

iii "[P]retty, docile words", "Come to my hand, and playful if I wish..." Do you think the poet has the power to control these words?

iv How do you think poets make "pets" out of some words?

v To which animals does the poet compare the pretty words? Are any of them dangerous? Why or why not?

Vocabulary

Similes

A **simile** is a figure of speech in which two things are compared, using the words **like** or **as**.

1 In this poem, the poet compares words to a number of different things. Make similes of your own to describe the following things.

i the wind ____________________

ii poetry ____________________

iii family ____________________

iv winter ____________________

v silence ____________________

vi ice cream ____________________

Further Discussion

1 The chapter "Why Books Are Dangerous" suggests that books can influence our day-to-day activities and behaviour. Do you think that some books should not be read because they will have a bad influence? Do you think the author believes this?

2 The writer of "Horsemail" implies that people no longer write letters on paper and send them by the postal service. Do you think this is true? Organise a debate in class comparing the merits of letters and emails.

3 In class, give examples of words that you think are "smooth", "tender", "bright" and "shy". What do you think makes them so?

Listening and Speaking

Your teacher will read out a poem. Note down all the adjectives you hear. Count them and find out how many you missed! Were any of them used in similes?

Learn More

The Pony Express was a system for delivering letters across America. How did your ancestors send each other messages in the past? Research and find out.

SCIENCE

"Any sufficiently advanced technology
is indistinguishable from magic."

—Arthur C. Clarke

13 When the Martians Landed

Andy Miller *is a writer and lives in England.*

When the Martians landed, they didn't look much like Martians. Do you remember? We watched it together—everyone did. We thought

there'd be **antennae**, the whole Bug-eyed Monster bit. My little brother wanted **tentacles**. We weren't expecting them to look like the prime minister. Nobody was.

The ramp extended from the silver spaceship and the band struck up the national anthem. The prime minister—the original one—straightened his tie and got ready to address the first Martian. It was a historic moment. He had prepared himself for anything, even tentacles. But when he looked up and saw himself walking down the ramp, right hand extended, famous smile in place, you could see the prime minister—our prime minister—was completely **flabbergasted**. Whereas the new PM—the Martian one, the alien—looked supremely confident. He looked like the one in charge.

There was an explanation. The Martians can change their appearance. If we humans saw them as they really were, they said, we would be **overwhelmed** by their ugliness and sliminess. It was important to build a relationship of trust early on. And so the two prime ministers waved to the cameras and walked off arm-in-arm to continue their discussions in private.

In the months that followed, more silver spaceships landed. The Martians offered to help us **eradicate** disease and **abolish** hunger. "Our new best friends," the prime minister called them. They **bombarded** us with wonderful Martian food—irresistible cakes and chocolate bars and crisps which tasted out of this world. All gifts, they said. "Eat up!" said the prime minister. "Eat up, you lovely people!" Everyone's been getting fatter. Even my little brother, though he's not so little these days. They've started talking about an "**obesity** opportunity" instead of a crisis.

Yesterday, the government announced a new exchange scheme for Earth children—a trip to Mars for anyone who tips the scales at fifty kilos, with a lookalike Martian to take your place while you're away. On TV, the prime minister smiled his famous smile and then—just for a second—I thought I saw him lick his lips. "You lovely people!" he said. I don't know about you, but suddenly I'm not feeling hungry.

---

antennae: long thin sensory appendages found in pairs on the heads of insects and some arthropods
tentacles: long slender appendage of an animal used for grasping or moving about
flabbergasted: greatly surprised
overwhelmed: overpowered, have a strong emotional reaction to
eradicate: remove or destroy completely
abolish: formally put an end to
bombarded: subjected to the continuous flow of something
obesity: grossly fat or overweight

Reading Comprehension

1 Answer the following questions.

i What did the narrator expect the Martians to look like? Why do you think he expected this?

ii Why was the prime minister flabbergasted?

iii What reason did the Martians give for changing their appearance to look like humans? Do you think they were telling the truth?

iv What form of help did the Martians give to the people of Earth?

v What was the "obesity opportunity" mentioned by the narrator? What was the Martians' attitude towards it?

vi What do you think was the Martians' real plan? What made the narrator suspicious?

Vocabulary

1 In the following sentences, the same word is used in different ways. Identify the words and what part of speech they take in each sentence. Do they sound the same if you read them out loud?

i a We will now present the chief guest with a bouquet.

____

b At present, I am too busy to take on any more work.

____

ii a The contents of the picnic basket smelled delicious.

____

b Nimit is not content with his current job.

iii a The rain fell continuously all day.

b I wish it would rain!

iv a We must arrange for some form of transport for the school trip.

b You'll need to transport all of those boxes to Mumbai.

v a Those three girls frequent the tennis club.

b We make frequent trips to my grandparents' house.

Grammar

Active and Passive Voice

The **active and passive forms** are two different ways of describing the same action.
In **active** sentences, the subject of the sentence is the person or thing *doing* the action and the object is the person or thing *receiving* the action.
For example: Anita threw away the piece of paper.

Anita	threw away	the piece of paper.
[subject]	[action]	[object]

In **passive** sentences, the subject is the person or thing *receiving* the action, and the person or thing *doing* the action may or may not be included.
For example: The piece of paper was thrown away by Anita.

The piece of paper	was thrown away	by Anita.
[subject]	[action]	

Or

The piece of paper	was thrown away.
[subject]	[action]

1 Circle the subject and underline the object in these active sentences.

i Mridula ate the oranges.
ii Samrat and Arun were playing with the ball.
iii Tanvi pushed the burglar into the pond.
iv Harinder sent the email to all her friends.
v Lightning struck twice.
vi Rocks rolled down the hillside.

2 Change the following sentences from passive to active form.

i The gold was stolen by Robin Hood.

ii Siddhartha was bullied.

iii That girl's name was forgotten by me.

iv The vase was broken by the tall man.

v These jalebis were bought by Ankit's father.

vi The apple was given to the teacher.

vii The letter was written by Supriya.

viii The ice cream had been eaten by the boys.

Writing

The narrator of the story was surprised that the aliens did not look as he had imagined them. Imagine an encounter with an alien. What would it look like? Where would it have come from? Write a descriptive paragraph about the alien.

Discussion

Do you think the author of this story is making any sort of comment on the modern world? If so, what is it?

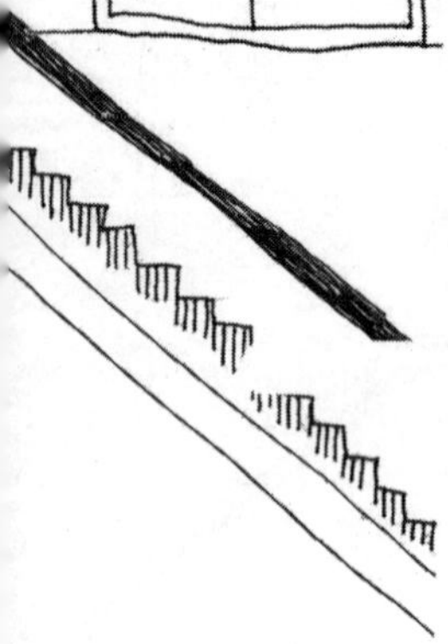

14 Elevators and Escalators

***Sampurna Chattarji** was born in Ethiopia. She is a poet, fiction writer and translator.*

Elevators and Escalators are cousins.
Elevators like listening to music.
Escalators don't.

Elevators are moody, they break down.
Sometimes the old ones—the ones
with the **grille** doors—get stuck between floors.
In movies, it's always the Elevator
that comes crashing down a zillion storeys,
ending in explosions of electricity and toasted hair.

And Escalators?

Escalators purr smoothly up and down,
secretly sticking out their tongues at their cranky, noisy,
disaster-prone, twice-removed cousins.

Elevators have men to run them.
The men sit on stools in uniforms
and press the buttons smartly
every time someone goes up or down.

Escalators are lonely.
No one runs them. They run on their own,
up and down, endlessly.
Escalators hate Elevators
when it comes to the question of men.

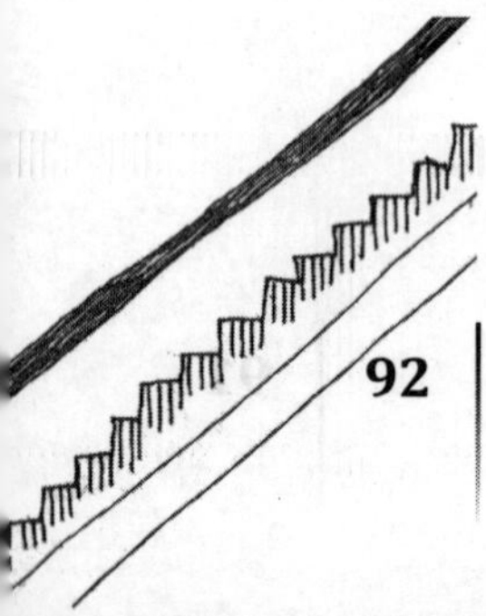

grille: grating or screen of metal bars or wires

Escalators know that there are two kinds
of humans on this planet.
The ones who are cowards
and the ones who are brave.

The brave ones *always* take the Escalator.

The scaredy-cats take the Elevator, not daring
to put their feet on the running treads,
they *dread* the fact that Escalators *never* stop,
except at night, when the malls are closed,
and even then they run, endlessly,
in the nightmares of the Elevator-people.

Escalators sneer at the Elevator-people.

Escalators are smooth and sly
and love those who love to glide,
love pointy painted toes,
love hems of shiny silk,
love soft and brushing hands.

Elevators are private. They hate crowds.
Takes only sixteen, you moron! they want to say
to the seventeenth person who squeezes in
at the very last moment.

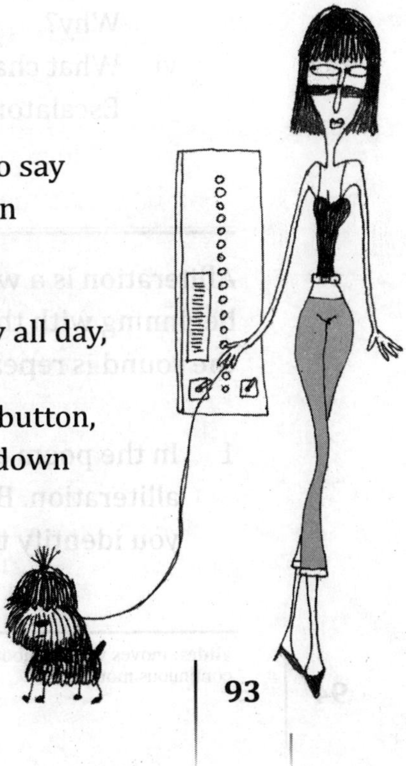

The Elevator's dearest wish is to be empty all day,
with no one but a little boy for company,
tall enough on tiptoe to reach the highest button,
small enough to know that riding up and down
is their shared idea of heaven.

The Escalator has no idea of heaven.
Its only wish is that short men
would stop wearing elevator shoes
and switch to escalator shoes instead.

Until that day arrives, it **glides** and **sneers**,
it runs and hates, while its cousin waits,
patiently, silently, for the doors to shut
and the sky to come a little closer.

Reading Comprehension

1 Answer the following questions.

i Why does the poet claim that "Elevators like listening to music"?

ii Why do Escalators hate Elevators?

iii Why are people afraid of Escalators?

iv Why does the poet call Elevators "private"?

v Do you think that the poet prefers Elevators or Escalators? Why?

vi What characteristics does the poet attribute to Elevators and Escalators?

Vocabulary

Alliteration is a way of writing (often used in poetry) in which words beginning with the same sound are placed close to each other so that the sound is repeated.

1 In the poem above, "explosions of electricity" is an example of alliteration. But there are some others in the poem as well. Can you identify them?

glides: moves with a smooth, quiet, continuous motion

sneers: contemptuous or mocking smile

2 You have already read the poem "Pretty Words" by Elinor Wylie. How many examples of alliteration can you find in that poem? Why do you think that poets use alliteration?

15 Science Star Omar

***Nick Arnold** is a writer who is best known for his* Horrible Science *series of books. This chapter is taken from the book* Suffering Scientists.

This chapter is about Ghiyath al-din Abu l'Fath Umar Ibn Ibrahim al-nisaburi al Khayyami. This is a bit of a mouthful and it must have taken ages for his mum to call him in for his tea.

Fortunately, he has gone down in history as...

Horrible Science Hall Of Fame: Omar Khayyam (AD 1048–1122)

Nationality: Persian

Omar was born in Khurasan in what is now Iran. Nothing is known about his family but the name Ibrahim means "tent maker" so maybe that's what his family did for a living. Young Omar must have had a good education because he became a teacher with an interest in scientific subjects. But he found it hard to study. He later admitted that as a teacher he was so busy teaching he had little time to find out about the subject he was supposed to be telling children about. Does your teacher have this problem—and dare you ask?

At least Omar managed to find time to write a book on algebra and another on music. Given a bit longer he might have written a book on musical maths!

A star is born

Around 1070 Omar made friends with an important judge Abu Tahir. The judge must have been into maths because Omar **dedicated** two more books on algebra to him...

Omar's work for the judge attracted the attention of the Sultan Jalal al-Din. And the Sultan gave Omar the job of looking after his astronomical **observatory**.

Omar was very happy and he spent the next eighteen years tracking the movements of over 100 stars. And this is how he made his... crucial calendar.

Seen from the earth, the stars seem to move around us during the year. By 1079 Omar had enough information from his stargazing to calculate the exact length of a year.

In fact, he was just 0.0002 days wrong. This meant that if you followed a calendar drawn up by Omar you'd find it was one day out in 5,000 years. Mind you, by then you might be too old to care too much even if you ended up missing your birthday or eating Christmas pudding on Boxing Day! (Our present calendar is actually less accurate than Omar's because it loses one day in 3,333 years.)

Omar advised the Sultan to **re-jig** the calendar to fit in with his newly calculated year. But then things began to go wrong.

First, the Sultan died.

Omar thought things could carry on because he was a pal of the

dedicated: exclusively assigned or allocated to
observatory: a room or building housing an astronomical telescope or other scientific equipment for the study of natural phenomenon

re-jig: rearrange

Grand Vizier—the Persian Prime Minister.

But the Sultan's queen seized power. She quarrelled with the Vizier and he was murdered by a mysterious killer.

Any friend of the Vizier wasn't exactly flavour of the month with the queen. Omar's **observatory** was closed down.

Omar wrote a book claiming that the ancient rulers of Persia were really nice people. Kind-hearted and generous—especially to astronomers like Omar.

But the queen was definitely not amused by this unsubtle hint and not surprisingly Omar was never given another job.

> ***Bet you never knew!***
>
> *Omar was an excellent poet and he is better known in Europe for his verse, rather than for his study of the uni-verse, ha ha.*

One of Omar's jobs was to draw up horoscopes based on the positions of the stars to foretell the future for important people. He wasted loads of time on this even though he secretly didn't believe in it. (Of course, people still believe in this practice, known as astrology, but you'd never catch a modern scientist peeping at their horoscope in the paper.)

Reading Comprehension

1 Answer the following questions.

i What difficulty did Omar face while teaching?

ii How did Omar obtain employment with the Sultan Jalal al-Din?

iii Was the calendar changed to reflect Omar's discovery? Why or why not?

iv Why did Omar write a book about the rulers of Persia? How did this affect his career?

v What can we deduce about Omar's childhood and family?

vi Why was the observatory closed down?

Vocabulary

1 Choose words from the box to match the meanings given below.

algebra	observatory	foretell	seize
subtle	supernova	annual	diurnal
crucial	agitate		

i To predict an event before it happens. ________

ii A branch of mathematics in which letters of the alphabet are used to represent unknown numbers. ________

iii Difficult to see. ________

iv Something that happens daily or during the day. ________

v To excite or disturb. ________

vi To grab or take hold of something forcefully. ____________

vii Necessary, or extremely important. ____________

viii The explosion of a star. ____________

ix Something that happens every year. ____________

x A building from which to observe the stars. ____________

Grammar

Conjunctions

Conjunctions are words and phrases that join together concepts and ideas.

For example: I bought you a cookie **but** I ate it.

In this sentence, the two concepts (buying a cookie and eating it) are linked by the word **but**.

There are several types of conjunctions.

Coordinating conjunctions are used to join parts of a sentence that are grammatically equal.

For example: I woke up early **but** was late for work.

Gorg **and** Quenk conquered the solar system.

Some coordinating conjunctions are: for, and, but, nor, or, yet, so.

Correlative conjunctions are made of two or more words, usually surrounding an adverb or adjective.

For example: **Either** she **or** her sister must have taken the book.

We don't know **whether** she would like pink roses **or** white ones.

You should buy **both** brown **and** white sugar.

Some correlative conjunctions are: either ... or, neither ... nor, not (only) ... but (also), both ... and, whether ... or

Subordinating conjunctions join clauses when one clause is dependent on the other.

For example: We went out for a walk **although** it was getting dark.

Brush your teeth **before** going to bed.

We were delayed **because** of the traffic.

Some examples of subordinating conjunctions are: although, after, because, as much as, as long as, so that, since, while, though, wherever, before, if, in order that.

1 Join the following using conjunctions.

i Jack went up the hill. Jill went up the hill.

____

____

ii I couldn't buy ice cream. I didn't have any money.

____

____

iii Raj didn't finish his math homework. Raj didn't finish his science homework.

____

____

iv You can travel on your holiday. You can stay at home.

____

____

v The weather was perfect. I did not go out.

____

____

2 Fill in the blanks using the correct conjunction from the brackets.

i ____________ Karthik ____________ Miriam has broken the vase. (either/or; both/and)

ii Smriti worked hard ____________ still failed the exam. (although; but)

iii Giri went out for a walk ____________ the blazing heat. (while; despite)

iv I can't visit my sister ____________ I save enough money. (until; because)

v We can attend the play ____________ we promise to behave. (as long as; although)

vi ____________ I don't like cabbage, this is very tasty. (wherever; while)

viii Pallav is learning Mandarin ____________ he may get a job in China. (as much as; in order that)

viii Yogendra was chosen as team captain ____________ he is the fastest runner. (because; before)

Further Discussion

1 "When the Martians Landed" is about aliens arriving on earth. Do you believe in the existence of aliens? Discuss with your class why you do or do not believe in them.

2 Do you think that technology is a good thing? Discuss the aspects of new technology that you like and dislike.

Learn More

1 Find out the names of some famous books or movies that deal with aliens from Mars. Have you seen or read any of them?

2 Omar Khayyam is known in Europe as a poet. He is most often associated with *The Rubaiyat of Omar Khayyam*, a collection of verses. Find out more about this book. What is the meaning of the title?

Listening and Speaking

Have you watched any movies or read any books that featured aliens? Give a short report about the book or movie to the rest of the class. Were the aliens friendly or not? How did they look? Discuss with your friends the way aliens are generally shown in movies.

NATURE

"In order to make an apple pie from scratch, you must first create the universe."

—Carl Sagan

16 The Caged Thrush Freed and Home Again

***Thomas Hardy** (1840–1928) was an English novelist and poet best known for his novels* Tess of the D'Urbervilles *and* Jude the Obscure.

"Men know but little more than we,
Who count us least of things **terrene**,
How happy days are made to be!

Of such strange tidings what think ye,
O birds in brown that peck and **preen**?
Men know but little more than we!

When I was borne from **yonder** tree
In bonds to them, I hoped to **glean**
How happy days are made to be,

And want and wailing turned to glee;
Alas, despite their mighty **mien**
Men know but little more than we!

They cannot change the Frost's **decree**,
They cannot keep the skies serene;
How happy days are made to be

Eludes great Man's **sagacity**
No less than ours, O tribes in **treen**!
Men know but little more than we
How happy days are made to be."

terrene: belonging to the earth
preen: to smooth or clean feathers with the beak
yonder: over there
glean: gather
mien: appearance
decree: a rule or an order
eludes: escapes
sagacity: wisdom
treen: trees

Reading Comprehension

1 Answer the following questions.

i "Men know but little more than we". What is this thing that men know little about?

ii Who is the speaker? Who do you think he or she is addressing?

iii What does the speaker mean by "who count us least of things terrene"? Why do men dismiss the birds?

iv What is the "mighty mien" that the speaker refers to?

Vocabulary

Prefixes

Prefixes are collections of letters that are placed at the beginning of a word in order to change the meaning. Some examples of prefixes are mis-, un-, en-, in-, im-, en-, dis-.

For example:

en + able = enable

un + known = unknown

dis + able = disable

in + exact = inexact

1 Add the prefixes in the box to the words given below in order to create new words.

mis-	un-	en-	in-	im-	en-	dis-

i understand ________

ii moderate ________

vi foreseen ________

vii advantage ________

iii regular ____________ viii grace ____________

iv connect ____________ ix necessary ____________

v perfect ____________ x rational ____________

2 "The Caged Thrush Freed and Home Again" is an example of a type of poem called a **villanelle**. In a villanelle there are only two rhyme sounds and the first and third lines are repeated alternately at the end of the stanza. Both lines are repeated at the end of the poem.
Have you read any other villanelles? Some examples are given below:
"Do Not Go Gentle into That Good Night" by Dylan Thomas
"The Ted Williams Villanelle" by Wendy Cope
"One Art" by Elizabeth Bishop
"Villanelle" by W.H. Auden
"The Story We Know" by Martha Collins

17 The Man Who Wanted To Fly

Ujwala Samarth is a writer, researcher and editor.

Characters

NARRATOR 1	NARRATOR 2	TRAVELLER
MAN	BIRD	STORY
PRIDE	HUMOUR	SATISFACTION
ANGER	HUNGER	THIRST
GREED	CURIOSITY	SORROW
HAPPINESS	LOVE	MEMORY

Scene 1

The scene opens with Traveller and the two Narrators on stage. They are sitting in firelight, in a forest clearing.

TRAVELLER: I guess you can't expect a banquet in the middle of a forest. Especially in a forest like this ... so dark and creepy. I'm glad I met you two. I wouldn't have liked to spend a night alone here.

NARRATOR 1: Oh, it's just the shadows that are frightening you. The forest is a safe place ... if you treat it with **caution** and respect.

NARRATOR 2: City-dwellers fear all the wrong things. I'd be far more frightened crossing one of those traffic-jammed roads in one of their hellish cities, than spending the night here. To most of us villagers, the forest is a good friend. Those shadows are—well, just shadows! Most of the time anyway ...

TRAVELLER: Oh you villagers! Always going on about how great your village life is. Clean air and being in touch with nature and all that

---

caution: to be careful

stuff! *(He hears a rustling noise and jumps up)* What's that? *What's that?*

Story is creeping across the edge of the stage, towards the firelight. She must look timid and weak. Her costume must rustle. Traveller and Narrators cannot see her yet.

NARRATOR 2: *(Listening)* What? Oh, that? Nothing to be frightened of, friend! Sit down, sit down! Either a snake or some small creature going on its **solitary** way or ... No wait ... that sounds like ... *(With growing excitement)* yes, I do believe ... I do believe that is a story! You know how stories like to gather around a warm fire on a dark night! What luck!

NARRATOR 1: Oh yes, stories just can't resist firelight. They're a little shy, though and won't always show themselves ... As you said, brother, what luck! Move up, city man, make space ... Make space for the story or it won't show itself. Now shh! Just wait, quietly.

(They all wait. Story creeps up and settles herself comfortably near the fire. Traveller cannot see her. Narrators and Bird can.)

TRAVELLER: Okay, so where is it, this story of yours? Or are you having me on? Making fun of the city-dweller, eh?

BIRD: *(Severely)* No one's making fun of you. Stories are serious business. But what do you know about stories?

Narrators look at each other, then at Story. They peer closely at her and seem reluctant to acknowledge her.

NARRATOR 2: It's *that* one, isn't it? The one with the sad ending?

Story holds out her hands to them, in a pleading gesture.

BIRD: Why are you hesitating, brothers? Do you want the story to die? It needs to be told! That's why it has come here—like an animal to the watering hole. Pass it on! Pass it on! Or watch it fade into nothingness.

---

solitary: alone

NARRATOR 1: Yes, it is looking rather forgotten and pale ... Yes, it *is* time to pass on the story once again ... perhaps. So that the mistakes are not repeated.

Story takes their hands and gets to her feet with a great effort. She leads them around the stage and back to Traveller. They come closer to Traveller, drawing his attention. Now he can see Story. He reacts as if he has seen a ghost. Story takes his hands in hers.

STORY: Listen, Traveller! Listen! Tell him, brothers—tell him, and save me.

NARRATORS: *(Together)* Listen!

NARATOR 1: This is a story about forgetting.

NARRATOR 2: A story about flying ...

NARRATOR 1: A story about flying ...

NARRATOR 2: And forgetting ...

NARRATOR 1: Forgetting and flying ...

Their words and voices sound like the wind blowing.

Scene 2

Scene changes to daylight as the voices echo softly, like the rustling of leaves or wings. Only Narrator 1 and Narrator 2 are on the stage.

NARRATOR 1: Long ago and far away, when people still had magic and could talk to their feelings, a man was walking through a forest.

Man enters. He carries a bundle and a stick.

NARRATOR 2: He sang softly to himself. He touched a leaf here, and a stone there. He called out to the animals. He felt the earth firm and **yielding** under his bare feet. How fine he looked!

NARRATOR 1: Yes, so fine!

NARRATOR 2: Coming to a river, he bent down, scooping up some water to drink ... He saw his own face in the deep, green water.

MAN: What a fine man I am. So handsome! So tall and strong! I am the reflection of all that is good and beautiful and wonderful on this earth!

Bird alights on a branch nearby.

NARRATOR 1: And then, he saw the bird, didn't he?

yielding: giving way

Narrator 2: Yes, he saw the bird! Oh I wish he hadn't looked up! I hate telling this part of the story!

Narrator 1: That's the trouble with you, isn't it? Always trying to give stories different endings, changing the way characters behave! Well, stories don't unfold like *that*. They won't change just to please you! He *did* see it, and what happened, *happened*.

Narrator 2: Yes, he looked up and he saw a bird sitting on a branch. It was beautiful, with a majestic beak and glossy feathers, preening itself in the sunlight! And then suddenly, it spread its wings and took off, off into the sky! The man caught his breath in awe. He watched the bird fly high up over the forest, watched it dip and dart and soar and dive ... He felt very small and heavy and sad.

Man is watching Bird fly. Bird may have a series of choreographed moves, set to some suitable music, to suggest flight.

Man: What is the use of being so handsome? I am tied to the earth! My beauty belongs up there with the sun and clouds and wind! I want to fly! I *will* fly! If I become lighter, then maybe I can fly. I must try to become lighter!

Narrator 1: So the man put down his bundle and his stick. He felt a little lighter ... Then, he took off his clothes ...

(Man takes off one layer of clothes.)

Man: Aah! I can feel the wind on my skin ... But, my hair slows me down ... It traps the wind. Maybe I need to cut it ... Or better still ... *(He takes a razor out from his bag.)*

Narrator 2: Then, he shaved off his hair and his beard and his moustache. And that was when someone could have stopped him from going any further, but no one did, no one did! Oh, it's entirely our fault, what happened to that fine young man—our fault!

Narrator 1: What's done is done! We weren't even there—no one was! Except for Bird, flying up in the sky. And what could *we* do anyway? Stop blaming *us* for the way the story goes—we're just storytellers!

MAN: Now, I am lighter, let me try flying! *(Man tries to fly. He stands on a rock and tries to get lifted by the wind. He runs and tries to take off.)* My feet will not lift! Why won't the wind carry me like a seed or a leaf? Why am I still so heavy?

(Man sits on the rock, and thinks deeply.)

MAN: I know! It is inside that I am still heavy! I have shed things on the outside, but inside I still carry so many things! Let me see what I have inside that I can throw away.

Each time Man throws his emotions on the stage, they appear in the form of actors. The act of 'throwing' the emotions out needs to be highly stylised and dramatic, accompanied by sound effects, or music to suit each emotion.

NARRATOR 2: He reached inside and took out Hunger and Thirst.

Man throws out Hunger and Thirst, who come rolling and falling on to the stage.

MAN: Hunger and Thirst! I do not need you! You are the source of all my troubles! I have to work and slave because of you! Be gone!

HUNGER: But ... I ensure that your body is **nourished!** You would have died if I hadn't reminded you to eat!

THIRST: And I remind you of your need for water, water to cool and clean your body.

MAN: I only know that Hunger and Thirst have made me miserable. When I don't satisfy you, I suffer! When I overindulge you, I suffer! Get lost!

Hunger and Thirst flee upstage, to a corner.

---

nourish: to supply with the food, water, etc.

NARRATOR 2: Next, he reached inside and took out Anger. *(Anger appears, like an angry cat, hissing and spitting. As Narrator speaks, it scratches Man's legs and arms. He wrestles with it and manages to throw it into the water.)*

ANGER: Throw me away, will you? Think you don't need me? Who gave you the strength to stand up against the man who wouldn't pay after you did his work? Who helped you to fight for your rights? Who gave you courage and ...

Anger struggles in the water.

MAN: All you ever did was cause misunderstanding and bitterness! You just would not let me tame you! Yes, okay you had your uses but I can do without you ... isn't that what all the great philosophers say?

He watches Anger drown.

NARRATOR 1: One by one, he took out all his feelings and emotions.

They appear on stage, as their names are called out and when they are pushed away, they go to a corner, upstage, and stand or sit or lie, looking defeated.

Narrator 1: Greed ...

GREED: You need me, sir, you need me. I am your ambition, your drive! Life would be so boring without a little bit of greed. It's always fun to have more ... and more ... and more ...

Man pushes Greed away.

NARRATOR 1: Satisfaction ...

SATISFACTION: How would you have known where to stop without me? That evil twin of mine, Greed would have driven you mad! You have thrown out Hunger, Thirst, Anger and Greed. Isn't that enough? Be satisfied now. Stop.

MAN: I will only be satisfied when I can fly! *(He pushes Satisfaction away.)*

NARRATOR 2: Curiosity ...

CURIOSITY: Don't you want to know what ...

MAN: Quiet! Curiosity, you are the biggest trouble maker of all! Ever since I was a small child you have caused nothing but trouble. Who encouraged me to look inside that beehive and got me stung? Who put the idea of reading my sister's diary into my head—I still have her bite marks on my arm! Who ...

CURIOSITY: Who led you to books and learning and discovery? Who opened your eyes to the wonders of the world? Anyway, go ahead! Throw me out! I'm quite curious to see how long before you are absolutely bored with your life!

NARRATOR 2: Next, he pulled out Humour.

HUMOUR: This is a joke, right? Oh come on, Man, you need a sense of humour in this grim world!

MAN: Oh all right, I'll keep a small piece of you. *(He breaks off a small piece of Humour.)*

HUMOUR: Ouch! That was *not* funny! *(He moves aside, nursing his wound.)*

NARRATOR 1: Pride, Sorrow, Happiness ... He reached inside and took them all out. *(Pride, Sorrow, Happiness all appear on stage. Sorrow and Happiness are clinging to each other.)* Man tried very hard to separate Sorrow and Happiness—he only wanted Happiness ...
(Man tries to pull Happiness away, but Sorrow will not let go.)

NARRATOR 1: But finally, he had to throw them both away because they would not be pulled apart.

Man pushes both away.

MAN: Go away! Shoo! *(He chases all the emotions off the stage.)* Now I feel better ... sort of empty, but ... free ... Now, let me see how light I am ... *(He tries to fly, but is unsuccessful. He sits down again, panting.)* No ... no, something is still keeping my feet on the ground.

NARRATOR 2: The man searched every corner of his mind and heart and body. Finally, his hands touched something warm and alive and pulsing ...

NARRATOR 1: Very **delicate** and strong ... He grabbed it in his fist and pulled it out!

Love and Memory are thrown on to the stage.

MAN: Who are you? What are you? How dare you hide like that?

MEMORY and LOVE: We ... we were frightened! Frightened for you! That's why we were hiding!

MAN: Frightened for me? Indeed! What are you?

LOVE: I am Love.

MEMORY: And I am Memory.

MAN: And why are you frightened for me?

MEMORY: Please listen. You need us. Don't throw us away. We have in our hands the seeds of all you have thrown out.

Love: We can make them all grow again...

MAN: After all the trouble I've taken to get rid of them!

MEMORY: Your feelings make you human! Without them, without us, you are like a drop of water that **evaporates** on a hot stone. Gone! Just like that!

LOVE: We bind you to other drops, we make you part of a river ...

---

delicate: very fine in quality

evaporate: to change from liquid into vapour, usually because of heat

Memory and Love: And the river gives you beauty and strength and courage. Don't you see? We make you part of the Whole.

Man: I see only that you make me heavy! Why do I need Love and Memory to fly? All I need to soar is to be empty! Is it the light, dry leaf that is carried on the wind or the heavy coconut? Once I am in the sky, with the whole world admiring my beauty and grace, why would I need to be part of any Whole? Stop snivelling and get lost!

Narrator 1: He grabbed Memory and Love and tried to throw them into the river. They clung to him.

Memory and Love: You need us, you need us! Stop! Listen! Please ...wait ...

Narrator 2: He struggled for a long time. Finally, he threw them screaming into the deep, deep water, where they sank slowly and painfully to the bottom.

Man stands with arms outstretched in the wind, but gradually he crumples up. He crouches by the river, growing smaller and smaller. During the lines above, Bird has come back to the branch. Traveller and Story are also back on stage. Story is tall and upright. Light dims.

Scene 3

Back to the opening scene, with Traveller, Narrators, Story and Bird around the fire.

Traveller: And so, did the man fly now that he had emptied himself of everything? He must have been lifted up by the slightest breeze!

Silence.

Traveller: Come on! Aren't you going to complete the story? Tell me what happened?

Narrators sit with their heads bowed in grief.

Narrator 1: *(With a deep sigh)* Bird, you were there.

Narrator 2: Yes, you tell him what happened.

Bird: When I returned to my branch, I looked for the beautiful, strong man but there was only a small, **hunched** stone in his place. *(Pause)* Oh, if only I had come back sooner! If only I had not been carried away

---

hunched: bent over

by the wind! I saw him down below as I was flying, admiring my flight and regretting his lack of wings. Then I saw him emptying himself of all that made him human and I came back to tell him this: only the memory of my branch and the love of my forest allow me to dare the sky ... Memory and Love are my true wings.

Reading Comprehension

1 Answer the following questions.

i Why do you think the second narrator claims the forest is safe "if you treat it with caution and respect"?

ii "Stories like to gather around a warm fire on a dark night". Comment.

iii Why is the story looking "forgotten and pale"?

iv Narrator 2 wants to change the ending of the story. Why does Narrator 1 object to this?

v Which were the most important feelings according to the Bird?

vi Do you think the role of the Traveller is important in this play? Describe this character.

vii Of which of his emotions did the man keep a small piece?

viii Do you think that this story could be staged easily? Why or why not?

ix "This is a story about a story." Comment.

Vocabulary

Synonyms

Synonyms are different words with similar or identical meanings.

1 For each of the following, choose the synonym from the words given in brackets.

i	solitary	(social	alone	quiet)
ii	choreograph	(direct	x-ray	edit)
iii	snivel	(shout	whine	laugh)
iv	delicate	(boorish	purple	ethereal)
v	brandish	(display	attack	burn)
vi	acknowledge	(comprehend	eviscerate	admit)

Grammar

Pronouns

Pronouns are words that can be used in place of a noun. They stop us from repeating the same word over and over.

Consider the following sentences:

I cannot find my ball. Have you seen my ball? My ball is red and blue and my ball is made of plastic.

When we replace **my ball** with the pronoun **it**, these sentences sound much better.

I cannot find my ball. Have you seen it? It is red and blue and it is made of plastic.

Personal pronouns stand in for people or things. Examples of personal pronouns are: I, me, you, we, they, she, he, him, her, us, it, them.

For example: I liked **her** speech.

Will **they** be meeting **us** next week?

He thought **it** was beautiful.

Demonstrative pronouns are used to indicate things that are near or far in the distance. Examples of demonstrative pronouns are: this, that, these and those.

For example: **This** bag is bigger than mine.

Those mountains are higher than **these**.

Interrogative pronouns are used to ask questions. Examples of interrogative pronouns are: who, whom, what, which, whoever, whatever and whichever.
For example: **Which** do you like better?
Whatever do you mean?
To **whom** shall I give this note?

1 Underline all the personal, demonstrative and interrogative pronouns in the following passage.

I ran down the corridor with the burglar close behind me. I turned left sharply at the end of the passage. He was unable to stop and stumbled through the doorway of the empty room. As quick as a flash I shut the door behind him and locked it. He was well and truly trapped.
I called the others and we questioned him through the locked door. We knew that this man's evidence could be crucial.
"Now," I said, "Who are you and why were you trying to steal the box?"
He pretended not to know what we were talking about.
"Which box? Whatever do you mean?"

Writing

Imagine you were the Traveller in this story. Write a short diary entry about your strange experience in the woods. Remember to put the date at the top of the entry and to write in the first person.

18 Life before the Dinosaurs

***Swagata Deb** and **Supriya Seshadri** are both scientists from IIT Delhi. Deb is a teacher and children's author. Seshadri is now involved in children's education. This chapter is taken from their book* Why We Are Where We Are.

The period from 570 million years ago (mya) to the present is divided into three eras: the Palaeozoic Era (570–245 mya), the Mesozoic Era (245–sixty five mya) and the Cenozoic Era (sixty five mya–the present). Dinosaurs lived and **flourished** in the Mesozoic Era. But what kinds of creatures lived before them? Did they live on land or water? What did they eat? How did they look? What happened to them?

At the beginning of the Palaeozoic Era (570–245 mya) although life forms were far more complex in structure than their single-celled ancestors, they still had simple, soft bodies. Over time these creatures started becoming more complex. Some evolved in order to get better at catching prey and some evolved so that they could protect themselves from predators. Some got strong limbs to move faster, while others developed shells to protect themselves. All the creatures in the beginning of this era lived in water. Towards the end of the Palaeozoic Era, a few evolved to be able to venture on to land.

Scientists have fossil records of an amazing number of creatures from the beginning of the Palaeozoic Era. A large number of different types of creatures evolved in a short period of time. So much so, that this event is popularly called the "Cambrian Explosion".

Of these, trilobites are a famous fossil group, probably next only to dinosaurs. These were creatures that had **jointed** legs, like insects and spiders. Trilobites had eyes, and some even had horns that were probably used for fighting. Then there was the pterygotus, a huge sea scorpion about seven feet long. It had six pairs of limbs and bulbous

flourish: to prosper or be successful

jointed: having joints

compound eyes! It was a deadly predator; it ate fish, trilobites and other creatures of the sea.

Earlier, fish had only round mouths that could suck food. Now, they developed bony jaws and teeth. Their tails and fins became strong and they could now move swiftly in the water. They developed **streamlined** bodies that helped them move fast. They were deadly, strong and powerful. Some of the most powerful among them were sharks, which dominate the waters even today!

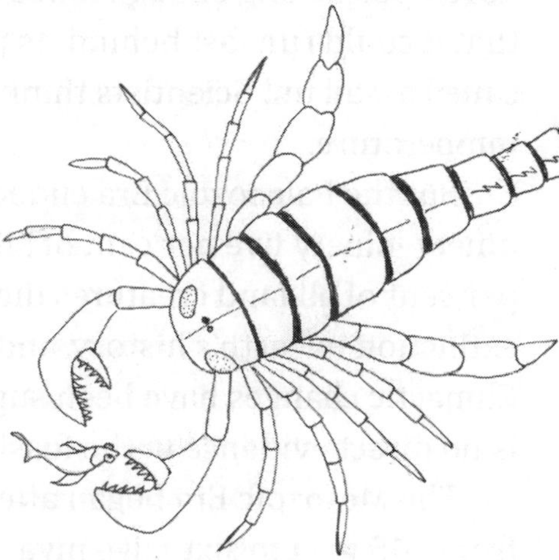

The earliest life forms on land were plants. Soon, **invertebrate** animals also began to live on land. In the beginning, very small creatures, like the ancient relatives of spiders and insects, started to live on land. Many were very tiny and lived off ancient plants. Scientists have found fossils of a prehistoric creature that closely resembles the dragonfly, which lived about 300 million years ago. It had a wing span of seventy centimetres. These are the largest known flying insects ever to have existed on earth. They ate other insects and small **amphibians**.

The first amphibians were the fish that crawled out of water in search of food. They were not fully equipped to move about on land because they still had fins. Their lungs were not developed enough for them to survive on land for long periods of time. As they evolved, they formed limbs and developed stronger lungs so that they could live on land as well as in water.

Next to evolve were reptiles. These were land animals in the true sense. They did not have to get back into water. They had strong limbs and well-developed lungs and could lay eggs on land. Reptiles soon began to dominate the land.

---

streamlined: shaped in such a way that moving in air or water is easy

invertebrate: without backbone
amphibians: creatures that can live both on land and in water

The dimetrodom was a **carnivorous** reptile. It was more than three metres long and could move very fast. This reptile had developed strong enough limbs to support its body weight. This meant that it could run fast behind its prey. It also had a giant fin on its back called a 'sail fin'. Scientists think that this fin helped to control its body temperature.

But the Palaeozoic Era ended with a massive extinction, where ninety–ninety five per cent of all water creatures and about seventy per cent of all land creatures died. This is probably the greatest extinction in earth's history, and no one really knows why it happened. Climactic changes have been suggested as a possible cause, but there is no direct evidence in the fossil record.

The Mesozoic Era began after the Palaeozoic Era and extended from 245 mya to sixty five mya. The first dinosaurs began to appear in the early period of the Mesozoic Era, called the 'Triassic Period'. Other creatures like frogs, turtles and mammals also appeared in this period, but in the Mesozoic Era, the dinosaurs dominated the land.

Reading Comprehension

1 Answer the following questions.

- i In which period did the dinosaurs flourish?
- ii What was the Cambrian Explosion? Why is it named thus?
- iii What were trilobites?
- iv How did fish evolve during this period?
- v What major event ended the Palaeozoic Era? Why did it happen?

2 State whether the following statements are true or false.

- i The Cambrian Explosion caused the extinction of many creatures. ☐
- ii All the creatures at the beginning of the Palaeozoic Era lived in water. ☐

---

carnivorous: meat-eating

iii The pterygotus was a harmless creature. ☐

iv The first life-forms on land were the amphibians. ☐

v The sail fin helped the dimetrodom to change direction while running. ☐

vi Reptiles could lay their eggs on land. ☐

Vocabulary

1 How many shorter words can you make from the following words?

i	dimetrodom	ii	pterygotus
iii	mesozoic	iv	invertebrate

Suffixes

Suffixes are groups of letters attached to the end of a word to change its meaning. Suffixes like **ation, ion, or, er** and **ment** can be used to change a verb into a noun.
For example: imagine → imagination
commence → commencement

2 Change the following verbs to nouns by using the suffixes given in the box below.

–ation – ion –or –er –ment

i	examine	________	ix	inform	________
ii	correct	________	x	write	________
iii	televise	________	xi	entertain	________
iv	congratulate	________	xii	animate	________

v edit	________	xiii move	________
vi conduct	________	xiv elevate	________
vii drive	________	xv relate	________
viii advertise	________		

Grammar

Possessive, Reflexive and Reciprocal Pronouns

Possessive pronouns indicate who owns something. Mine, yours, his, hers, ours, theirs and its are examples of possessive pronouns.

For example: Meenakshi's story was exciting, but **yours** was funnier.

Jai asked if he could borrow my watch since he had lost **his**.

Reflexive pronouns are used to refer back to the subject of the sentence or clause. Myself, yourself, himself, herself, itself, oneself, ourselves, yourselves and themselves are examples of reflexive pronouns.

For example: At the party, the sisters stayed in one corner and talked quietly among **themselves**.

I hurt **myself** this morning when I tripped and fell in the garden.

You need to have confidence in **yourself**.

Reciprocal pronouns are used when each of two or more subjects are acting in the same way towards the other(s). Each other and one another are examples of reciprocal pronouns.

For example: The pirates all betrayed **one another** and were easily caught.

The twins gave **each other** presents on their birthday.

1 In the following sentences, underline the pronouns and identify their types.

i My brothers are very fond of one another.

____

ii She was willing to laugh at herself for being so foolish.

____

iii Unless you and your friend Shikha apologise to each other, you'll make yourselves very miserable.

____

iv The house on the corner is mine.

____

v Since the dog has helped himself to your cake, would you like to share ours?

____

vi Just keep telling yourself that it will be over soon.

____

vii The homesick children cried themselves to sleep on the first night.

____

viii Though we hated each other at first, we soon found ourselves to be good friends.

____

Further Discussion

1 Both "The Caged Thrush Freed and Home Again" and "The Man Who Wanted To Fly" are about birds. Do you think the birds in the two chapters are similar?

2 In "The Man Who Wanted To Fly", which of the man's feelings and emotions do you think were most important? Why?

Learn More

1 Find out everything you can about these well-known types of dinosaur. In what periods did they appear?

i Stegosaurus
ii Archaeopteryx
iii Tyrannosaurus Rex
iv Megalosaurus
v Diplodocus

Listening and Speaking

1 Prepare a short speech on the subject of protecting the environment. What do you think are the biggest threats to the environment? How can we avoid them? Deliver your speech to the class.

SPORTS

"I always turn to the sports section first. The sports page records people's accomplishments; the front page has nothing but man's failures."

—Earl Warren

19 The Trial

***Dan Freedman** is a football editor and fan who lives in England. This chapter is from his book* The Kick Off.

Jamie knows he has to play well in this trial match if he wants to get into the football team. But then everything seems to go horribly wrong ...

Marsden handed Jamie the ball.

Jamie looked around. None of the others on his team had made a move to take the **penalty**. It had to be him.

Jamie knew it wasn't just the keeper that he was up against now. It was every other player on the pitch. Not even his own teammates wanted him to score. Why would they? They all wanted to get into the A team just as badly as he did. Why would they want him to steal all the **glory** in the last minute?

Jamie reached down and placed the ball on the spot. He could feel his heart thudding as he put the ball down.

"Make sure you don't MISS," hissed Dillon, standing between Jamie and

penalty: in football, an opportunity to score a goal when the opposing team breaks a rule
glory: praise

the goal. He was so close that Jamie could see the little droplets of spit coming out of his stinking mouth as he spoke.

Jamie fended Dillon's heavy frame out of the way. He needed to concentrate. He wanted to be **decisive** but thousands of questions were all closing in on him at once: Power or placement? To the side? It might go wide. Straight down the middle? The keeper will save it.

Mr Marsden raised the whistle to his mouth. The burst of noise was the signal for Jamie to step forward.

"I can't miss, I can't miss," he said to himself as he walked towards the spot, head bowed.

Everything went completely blank.

Jamie saw his feet run up to the ball but somehow felt unable to control them. His mind and body were disconnected from each other. He was taking the penalty but he had no idea what he was actually going to do with it.

Then something very unlucky happened.

As Jamie moved to strike the ball with his left foot, his right foot went over a **divot** in the pitch, twisting his ankle right over.

It threw Jamie off balance completely. He started to fall over. He should have stopped, got himself together and taken another run-up. But he didn't. He still tried to take the penalty.

As he was falling, he flung his foot towards the ball so desperately, so violently, that his left boot actually flew off his foot.

It shot right up into the air.

Jamie yelled out in horror.

His boot rocketed skywards, doing somersaults as it went. Meanwhile, the ball that should have been flying into the back of the net was rolling slowly and painfully along the ground towards the goalkeeper's waiting hands.

This was his worst nightmare. All the players on both sides were laughing. At him.

"That's the worst penlty I've ever seen! You're rubbish!" Dillon shouted, pointing straight at Jamie.

---

decisive: settling an issue quickly and effectively

divot: a small hole in the ground

Jamie's blood was boiling with rage, embarrassment and frustration. The sight and sound of Dillon's stupid, ugly, disgusting laugh was too much to take.

He shoved Dillon hard in the chest and walked away.

"Aaah," cried Dillon dramatically. He stumbled backwards and fell to the ground clutching his neck.

Jamie couldn't believe what Dillon was doing. He was actually faking it. He was pretending Jamie had punched him!

"Johnson, come here," said Marsden beckoning Jamie with his finger. His voice was serious.

"You're not falling for that, are you, sir? He's taking the ____"

"I'm not falling for anything." Marsden reached for his pocket.

"Sir! I didn't do anything!"

"Yes, you did, Jamie. I know you're upset about the penalty but you raised your hands to an opponent and you can't do that on a football pitch."

Marsden **brandished** the red card above his head so everyone could see.

Jamie had been sent off.

KINGFIELD SCHOOL UNDER 14s TRIAL MATCH FULL-TIME RESULT	
BLUES **1** Walsh 12	REDS **0** Johnson Missed Pen. 61 Johnson sent off 62

brandished: waved or flourished as a threat or in anger or excitement

Reading Comprehension

1 Answer the following questions.

i Why weren't Jamie's teammates supporting him?

ii Why do you think Dillon came up to speak with Jamie before the penalty?

iii Why didn't Jamie stop and retake the penalty after he tripped?

iv What happened when Jamie kicked the ball?

v Do you think Mr Marsden realised that Dillon was faking his injury? Why did he send Jamie off?

vi What caused the other players to laugh at Jamie?

vii What sort of person was Dillon? Describe his character.

viii Do you think that Mr Marsden made the right decision?

Vocabulary

1 Do you know the meanings of these metaphors about sports? Discuss what they might mean and which sports they may have originated from.

i a level playing field ____________________

ii on the ropes ____________________

iii not cricket ____________________

iv stalemate ____________________

v a knockout blow ____________________

vi move the goalposts ____________________

vii a dark horse ____________________

viii only a pawn in the game ____________________

Grammar

Clauses

Clauses are parts of a sentence that consist of a subject and a predicate. As you have already learnt, the predicate is the part of a sentence or clause which tells us something more about the subject.

There are three types of clauses.

Main clause: This type of clause has a subject and a verb which together form a complete thought. ***For example***: "My friend (subject) is (verb) tall" is a complete thought, since it makes sense by itself.

Subordinate/dependent clause: These clauses are made up of a subordinate conjunction, a subject and a verb. Together they form an incomplete thought. ***For example***: "If (subordinate conjunction) you (subject) are (verb) busy" does not form a complete thought, since it needs another clause to be added to it in order to make sense. Similarly "because my father is singing" is not a complete thought.

Subordinate clauses need to be added to a main clause, since they cannot stand alone as complete sentences.

For example: If you are busy I can come back later.

If you are busy	I can come back later.
[subordinate clause]	[main clause]

My sister is covering her ears because my father is singing.

My sister is covering her ears	because my father is singing
[main clause]	[subordinate clause]

Relative clause: These clauses begin with a relative pronoun or relative adverb. Clauses which begin with who, whom, whose, which, that, when, where, why or how are relative clauses. These cannot stand alone and have to be combined with a main clause.

For example: "Which my brother likes" or "That was warm" are not complete thoughts. "That is the restaurant which my brother likes" or "The cat chose the cushion that was warm" are complete thoughts and can stand alone as sentences.

1 Create main clauses of your own to make full sentences with the subordinate clauses given below.

i Since she had forgotten her homework

____

ii If Kiran is not careful

____

iii Which you were probably saving for breakfast

____

iv When you forget your best friend's birthday

____

v Because I'm too tired

____

vi Whose house it was

____

vii Although she only came to visit once a year

____

2 Circle the main clause and underline the subordinate clause in the following sentences.

i Simran is angry because Yamini forgot to buy the milk.

ii After we had finished lunch, Ravi took us all out for ice cream.

iii Daisy is scared of our dog Julius even though he is really friendly.

iv Once I turn fifteen I'll be allowed to stay out till eleven o'clock.

v While others were carrying their books, Maansi was carrying her tanpura.

vi We were asked to wait until Dr Raina had finished seeing his patients.

vii Remember to collect your coat and bag before leaving.

viii We waited for hours before the concert finally started.

3 Fill in the blanks in the following sentences containing relative clauses.

i Kate screamed ______________ she saw the huge spider on her desk.

ii Akshay, ______________ was in a bad mood, told Shweta to go away.

iii Isn't that the man ______________ stole your handbag?

iv He refused to meet his friends, ______________ struck me as very strange.

v I met Abhijit ______________ he visited Kolkata two years ago.

vi Leela tripped over the ball ______________ had rolled into the garden.

vii Tara apologised to the vendor ______________ cart she had hit.

viii That is the monkey ______________ stole my peanuts!

Writing

Write about an incident when you felt really disappointed about something.

Discussion

Do you think that what happened was Jamie's fault? Give reasons for your answer.

20 The Spirit of Cricket

***Sunil Gavaskar** is a former cricketer and captain of the Indian cricket team. He has written four books on cricket:* Sunny Days, Idols, Runs n' Ruins *and* One Day Wonders. *This speech is from the MCC Spirit of Cricket Cowdrey Lecture delivered on 29 July 2003.*

Will we ever get the likes of Sir Garfield Sobers and G.R. Vishwanath again? That greatest of cricketers, Gary Sobers, not only indicated more than once to umpires that he had caught the ball on the bounce but also declared his innings closed once in a test match in spite of having two of his main bowlers injured and left a challenging target. If a captain does that today, of course, the Anti-corruption Unit of the ICC would be breathing down his neck, but all Gary wanted was to **enliven** a dead series.

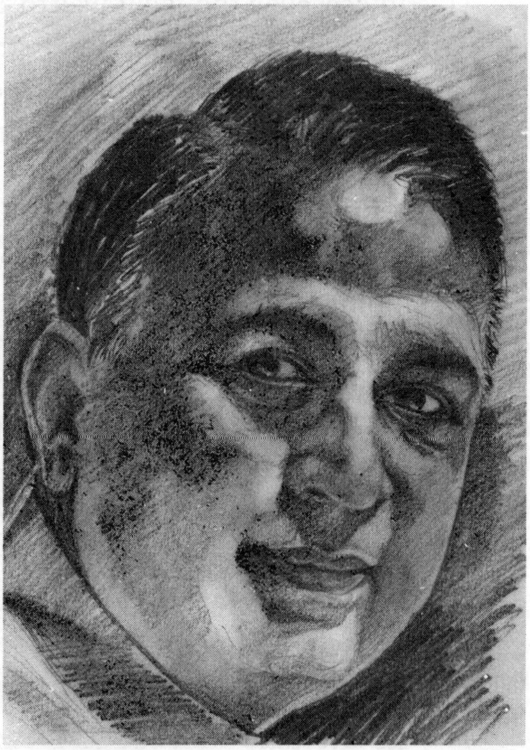

G.R. Vishwanath was the captain who recalled Bob Taylor when he was given out by the umpire. Bob's bat had brushed the pads, which had misled the umpire into giving him out caught behind. Like the true sportsman he is, Vishy walked up to the umpire and politely withdrew the appeal. India lost the test, but Vishy is remembered for that and loved all the more for it.

Today, thanks to the win-at-all-costs theory, appeals are made even though the fielders know that the batsman is not out. There is the other side, of course, where a batsman knows he is out but stays put and

enliven: make more entertaining or interesting

rubs some other part of his body if it's an appeal for a catch or shows his bat if there's an appeal for lbw. The rewards have become high, and rightly so, but it has to a great extent taken away from the spirit of the game, where bowlers applauded a good shot and batsmen acknowledged with a nod a good delivery from a bowler who beat them. While today, in order not to give any **psychological** advantage to the opposition, there's hardly any applause from the fielding side when a batsman reaches a fifty or a century.

It's hard to understand how applauding **concedes** any advantage to the batsman, but we see it increasingly where, **barring** the odd fielder, the others **feign** total ignorance of the batsman reaching a landmark.

This is in stark contrast to my first series in the West Indies, where one could sit with the greats like Gary Sobers, Rohan Kanhai and Lance Gibbs at the end of a day's play and ask them about batting and how to improve. They were more than happy to give good sound advice, even though it was to an opponent and could be used against them the next day to their team's **detriment**. It wasn't that these great cricketers did not want their team to win. It was just the fact that they believed that helping an opponent only produced good cricket and was good for the game.

How about the England team under Norman Yardley raising three cheers for Don Bradman when he came out to play his last test innings? Such a gesture is unthinkable today where the opponents hardly greet each other and if there's anything to say it's invariably not very pleasant. The thinking is that with the stakes being so high, any friendly **overture** takes away from the competitiveness of the player.

Today, though there is a Code of Conduct, the verbal bouncers go on pretty much unchecked and, unless something is done quickly about it, the good name of the game that we all know will be mud. Just look at any school game anywhere in the world and we will see bowlers having a go at the batsman. They see it on TV from their heroes and believe that it is a part of the game, and so indulge in it.

---

psychological: affecting or arising out of the mind, related to the mental and emotional state of a person
concede: finally admit or agree that something is true
barring: except for
feign: pretend
detriment: the state of being harmed or damaged
overture: an approach made with the aim of opening negotiations or establishing a relationship

Here it is crucial for the coaches to step in and tell them, while the kids are at an impressionable age, that this is wrong and cricket has been played for years without indulging in personal abuse. Maybe we should tell TV producers that, just like they don't show any of the streakers at the ground anymore, they should not show close-ups of players verbalising each other. With the cameras being so good, it is easy to lip-read and kids can see that it is not the Bible nor the Koran nor the [Bhagvad] Gita which is being quoted on the field.

The sad part is that very little is being done about it. If a player even so much as glares at the umpire or stays a micro-second longer at the crease after being given out, he is hauled up and in trouble. If there is protection for the umpire from the players, why not protection to players from abusive players?

... Let me end by repeating part of what Sir Don Bradman said about the game. We are all custodians of the game, and the game will prosper if we can leave it better than we found it. It is something that we must all endeavour to do—and it is achievable if we work sincerely towards it. I am confident that we can do it and when—and not if—we do it, then Colin [Cowdrey] sitting up there with the gods will smile and say, "Well done, chaps—that's the spirit."

Reading Comprehension

1 Answer the following questions.

- i Why does Gavaskar remember Sobers and Vishwanath fondly?
- ii Why did Sobers, Kanhai and Gibbs give Gavaskar advice?
- iii What did Norman Yardley's team do? Does Gavaskar think a modern team would do this?
- iv What would Gavaskar like the TV producers to stop showing? Why?
- v How are the actions of famous cricketers influencing the behaviour of children?

vi Does Gavaskar feel that the Code of Conduct has helped the situation? Give reasons for your answer.

vii "The rewards have become high". How has this changed the game?

viii What instructions does Gavaskar suggest giving to the TV producers? Why?

ix Can a player be rude to the umpire?

Vocabulary

1 Find words or phrases from the text that mean the following.

i to fake ______________

ii a caretaker ______________

iii to be forced to account for one's behaviour, or be punished.

____

iv to criticise strongly ______________

v concerning the mind ______________

vi to try to achieve something ______________

vii necessary ______________

viii constantly ______________

ix acknowledge the truth of something ______________

x completely different ______________

Grammar

Noun Clauses

Noun clauses are clauses that function as nouns. ***For example***: in the sentence "**What Gautam did** was wrong", **what Gautam did** is the subject of the sentence, and so it acts like a noun.

1 Underline the noun clauses in the following sentences.

i I don't know who to ask for help.
ii Kamini's problem was that she had a terrible temper.
iii I hope her brother knows how to cook.
iv None of us knew that Samrat couldn't swim.
v What Simardeep did was very rude.
vi Do you know where the bus stand is?

Further Discussion

1. "Sticks and stones may break my bones but words can never hurt me". Both the chapters in this section are about verbal taunts on the sports field. Do you think that such behaviour should be banned? Do you agree with Sunil Gavaskar that it is harming the game?

2. In his speech, Gavaskar suggests that young children playing sports are influenced by the behaviour of the cricketers they see on the television. Do you feel that you are influenced by what you see on television? Organise a debate in class on the subject.

Listening and Speaking

Your teacher will read out a passage about a famous cricketer. Listen closely and try to write down the important details of his life, including date of birth, the team he plays for, and why he is famous.

Acknowledgements

The publishers would like to thank the following authors, illustrators and publishers for permission to use their materials:

Nury Vittachi for "In the Playground" from *Twilight in the Land of Nowhen* (Scholastic India: 2008); Paro Anand for "Dear Dad" from *School Ahead* (Scholastic India: 2006); Vandana Singh for "A Martian Homecoming" from *Seven Science Fiction Stories* (Scholastic India: 2006); Scholastic UK for "The Date for Reform" from *Julius Caesar and His Foul Friends* by Toby Brown (Scholastic UK: 2006); "When the Martians Landed" by Andy Miller from *Wow! 366*: Speedy Stories in Just 366 Words (Scholastic UK: 2008); "Science Star Omar" from *Suffering Scientists* by Nick Arnold (Scholastic UK: 2000); "The Trial" from *The Kick Off* by Dan Freedman (Scholastic UK: 2007); Devika Rangachari for "Rajyasri and Her Brothers" from *Harsha Vardhana* (Scholastic India: 2009); Neil Gaiman for "Why Books are Dangerous" from *Guys Write for Guys Read* edited by Jon Scieszka (Viking: 2005); Siddhartha Sarma for "Horsemail" from *103 Journeys, Trips, Voyages and Stuff* (Scholastic India: 2009); Sampurna Chattarji for "Elevators and Escalators" from *The Fried Frog and Other Funny Freaky Foodie Feisty Poems* (Scholastic India: 2009); Ujwala Samarth for "The Man Who Wanted to Fly" from *Plays for Schools* (Scholastic India: 2007); Swagata Deb and Supriya Seshadri for "Life Before the Dinosaurs" from *Why We Are Where We Are* (Scholastic India: 2009); the M.C.C for "The Spirit of Cricket" by Sunil Gavaskar from *The Scholastic Book of Historic Speeches* edited by Arunava Sinha (Scholastic India: 2006); Taposhi Ghoshal for the illustrations for "In the Playground", "The Schoolboy" and "The Sea"; Anjali Nayar for the illustrations for "Horsemail" and "The Caged Thrush Freed and Home Again"; Baaraan Ijlal for the illustrations for "Pretty Words" and "The Man Who Wanted to Fly"; Priya Kuriyan for the illustrations for "Ozymandias" and "Elevators and Escalators"; Zainab Tambawalla for the illustrations for "Rajyasri and Her Brothers" and "The Spirit of Cricket"; Kunal Kundu for the illustrations for "Dear Dad", "Why Books are Dangerous" and "When the Martians Landed"; Nilima Eriyat for the illustrations for "Brother and Sister"; Shweta Mohapatra for the illustrations for "A Martian Homecoming"; Garima Gupta for theme page art.

While every attempt has been made to trace copyright holders for the text and illustrations, this has not been possible in all cases. Any omissions brought to our attention will be rectified in future editions.

Evaluation Table

Name: ____________________

Date: ____________________

THEME	Comprehension	Grammar, Spelling and Punctuation	Vocabulary	Organisation of Ideas	Making Connections	Expression
Growing Up						
Family						
History						
Words						
Science						
Nature						
Sports						